Natives & Newcomers

Challenges of the Encounter

Cabrillo Historical Association aids and promotes the historical, educational, interpretive, and scientific activities of the National Park Service and Cabrillo National Monument. As a nonprofit co-operating association authorized by Congress, it publishes and distributes interpretive information to park visitors and the general public. Chartered in 1956, the Cabrillo Historical Association is governed by a volunteer board of directors.

Cabrillo Historical Association
P.O. Box 6670, San Diego, California 92166

Production coordination: Sara Gotthold, Tricia Takacs

Graphic design: Penina & Associates

Published by the Cabrillo Historical Association
San Diego, California, 1993

ISBN 0-941032-05-1

Printed on recycled paper.

Natives & Newcomers

Contents

MAPS

Introduction

Alfred W. Crosby, arguably the premier historian of the encounter, has pointed out, in the final paper of this collection, that "calories can make as much history as cannon." Indeed, the statistics he provides suggest that calories in fact have made as much history as cannon. This phrase can act as a touchstone for this publication of four of the five papers presented during the series "Natives and Newcomers: Challenges of the Encounter." The colonial imperative, crossing the Atlantic, and building careers are the other touchstones to history that here celebrate the historian's craft.

In the fall of 1991, in anticipation of two events important to Cabrillo National Monument and to world history, the Cabrillo Historical Association launched a five-part seminar series extending through 1992. These Sunday afternoon public seminars featured five prominent historians. They considered a number of less discussed aspects of the encounter of peoples, plants, and pests during that fateful period of a half millennium ago. The two historical events that occasioned the creation of the series included a commemoration of the quincentennial year of the Columbian voyages and the recognition of the 450th anniversary of the exploration by European peoples of the west coast of what would become the United States. We remember Columbus in a global sense; we remember locally Juan Rodriguez Cabrillo (or João Rodrigues Cabrilho) for his landing in San Diego Bay in 1542. Both adventurers, and those who followed, were from across a distant sea. And so the purpose of the lecture series was to "re-examine changes across the Atlantic during the Age of Exploration."

Cabrillo Historical Association, a cooperating association of the National Park Service, and Cabrillo National Monument co-sponsored the series. As is evidenced by the four papers that make up this festschrift, consideration is given to concerns of calories, colonies, crossings, and careers. There is a distinct shortage of commentary on cannon. Many other publications have, over the centuries, catered to the military history of the encounter, or, as is more truthful, the conquest. The pages that follow are given over much more to concerns of social history. As well, the focus has been global with regard to the Age of Discovery, concentrating not on Cabrillo, but upon his age. *Cabrillo's World: A Commemorative Edition of Cabrillo Festival Historic Seminar Papers* (Cabrillo Historical Association, 1991) is a recommended companion volume to this current collection.

Initiating the "Natives and Newcomers" series on October 13, 1991, Dr. Roger Cunniff, of San Diego State University, considered the "Demographics and Lifeways of Native Americans Prior to European Contact." His presentation (done orally and not reproduced here) was an appropriate beginning for the series as it laid the groundwork for greater appreciation of the profound effects that European peoples would have upon the Western Hemisphere. By the conclusion of the series, the effects of the Americas upon Europe, the other side of the "changes across the Atlantic" coin, would be detailed by Dr. Crosby. The exchange of "plagues and peoples" and crops and calories would profoundly affect the world, fully united only during these past five centuries. The pages that make up this reading adventure that you are about to take provide us with information about aspects of the lesser known worlds of colonization, career building, calorie sources, and crossings aboard Spanish ships.

While we may have a romanticized concept of the colonization of "New Spain," a view of a uniform advance, especially northward out of Mexico, Dr. Gilberto Hinojosa dissuades us of this incorrect idea. In his January 12, 1992, address this University of Texas (San Antonio) scholar makes the convincing case that at least four independent surges occurred northward into the southern tier of the latter-day United States. In both time and space, these colonial thrusts out of the Valley of Mexico were each possessed of a very different character. An ever-varying combination of racial and social groups leap-frogging northward in each of the four waves met conditions, lands, and peoples unique to each isolated corridor. The times and purposes of each incursion, whether to latter-day New Mexico, Texas, California, or Arizona, were not to be repeated exactly in any one or another of these four migrations. The fluidity of movement within and between social and racial groups of the era of colonization was quite extraordinary. Dr. Hinojosa chronicles a societal structure not in keeping with our preconceived notion of Spanish rule in the "new world" aborning in the sixteenth through nineteenth centuries.

Being there, in the tumult of a land where castes and color were ever chameleonic, was one thing; getting there was quite another. Dr. Carla Rahn Phillips, of the University of Minnesota, told us, on April 5, 1992, just how demanding the voyage across the Atlantic could be. "The Spanish Maritime Experience" has been dealt with by a number of authors who have evidenced a special interest in ships and navigation. And while Dr. Phillips does not overlook these essentials in the maritime experience, as with our other authors, she delves into the social history of those who crossed the sea into a new world. Visions of biscuit laced with weevils, or worse, flood our mind's eye when we attempt to imagine a trans-Atlantic voyage in the sixteenth century. Privations, plagues, and problems of all sorts seemed commonplace on such trips. But,

and much to the surprise of most readers, we find that nutrition aboard many of these crossings was not nearly so harrowing. Indeed, the calories consumed by many a seaman rivaled, or often surpassed, a sod-bound farmer of the era. Dr. Phillip's story, like those of the other writers here, focuses upon literature sources less often tapped—and which lead to some very different conclusions from those uncritically accepted to now.

In the crisp and concise style for which Dr. Iris Engstrand is locally known in Southern California, we learn of the career that "José Longinos Martínez, the First European Naturalist in San Diego" forged for himself as he traveled both Baja and Alta California. Dr. Engstrand's lecture of July 19, 1992, followed the naturalist Longinos Martínez as he discovered medicinal plants, native American tribes yet unknown to the Spanish powers, and other aspects of natural history that have remained unremarked upon by other historians. Dr. Engstrand, as a professor of history at the University of San Diego, is not only one of the leaders of the local history community, but a force in Renaissance-era Spanish history on a global scale. She correctly points out that the Royal Scientific Expedition of the fin de siècle, and finally extended into 1803, should have led to a greater contribution to the understanding of American natural history in Europe. A greater role for the Spaniards in the "patronage of natural history was left to a future generation" because the "Napoleonic wars commanded the attention of Carlos IV." Once again, this author has dug deeply and found lesser-known sources with which to provide us with yet more understanding of colonial social history.

In the fifth and final lecture (the fourth paper in this collection), Dr. Alfred Crosby, of the University of Texas at Austin, dealt with the impact in Europe of the voyages of exploration. Presented on September 27, 1992, just one day short of the 450th anniversary of Cabrillo's entry into San Diego Bay, Dr. Crosby's seminar reminded the standing-room-only audience that it was calories, not cannon, that in the end remade the world. Not unlike the immensely successful Smithsonian Institution's examination of five "seeds of change" (maize, potatoes, sugar, horses, and disease), Dr. Crosby chose to discuss the impact of maize and potatoes on European history. Indeed, Dr. Crosby was a major consultant to the Smithsonian and recognized the spectacular importance of these two crops to the sweep of world history. Like William H. O'Neill before him, Crosby prefers to ask grand questions: "Could there have been an industrial revolution in northern Europe without the potato?" He has an answer; a reading of his persuasive essay will provide you with, shall we say, food for thought!

The Cabrillo Historical Association provides aid to the National Park Service in its mandate to both protect and interpret the scenic, scientific, cultural, and historic resources in its charge. The sale of this and other publications of this non-profit association make possible lecture series such as "Natives and Newcomers." Your support of the Cabrillo Historical Association is appreciated.

Donald J. McGraw MS, Ph.D.
Chair, CHA Board of Directors
Chair, "Natives and Newcomers"
Lecture Series

In this selection, Professor Gilberto Hinojosa of the University of Texas at San Antonio examines race and class in New Spain and along New Spain's northern frontier. Dr. Hinojosa specializes in the history of Borderlands and the Southwest. His publications include Tejano Origins in Eighteenth Century San Antonio *(co-edited with Gerald E. Poyo, 1991),* Viva la Virgen de Guadalupe! A History of Our Lady of Guadalupe Parish *(co-authored with Mary Ann Bruni, 1988),* They Still Call It Home *(1985),* Laredo, Texas: A Gateway Community in the Texas Borderlands *(co-authored with William J. Foley, Idys Wayne Cox, and Anne A. Fox, 1984), and* A Borderlands Town in Transition: Laredo, 1755-1870 *(1983).*

Class and Race in Borderlands Societies

AN INTERPRETATIVE ESSAY

Gilberto M. Hinojosa

OMMUNITIES in New Spain's northern frontier displayed a dynamic social structure that allowed a considerable amount of mobility. As in the rest of the colony, social rank in the northern frontier was described by racial designations, yet position in society was not limited by race, since the ongoing *mestizaje*, or racial mixture, prevented clear and firm racial distinctions. Intermarriage, inclusion in the Church, and very importantly periodic economic expansion provided incorporation into society for various groups and in some instances facilitated an upward mobility expressed in racial "passing," or changing of designations, that created a dynamic society.

Racial/class categories appeared simple on the surface, but were in fact quite complicated. Generally, Hispanic settlers were called *gente de razón* (those with the use of reason) to distinguish them from the *indios* (the Indians), who were not accorded full rights as citizens. Among the Hispanics, the elites were designated *españoles*, or Spaniards, but very few were actually from Spain and in most instances their Spanish ancestry was vague after generations in the New World. The Indian designation was clearly more racially-determined than "Spanish," but being "Indian" had a variety of meanings. There were, for example, *indios bárbaros* ("barbaric" or warlike, nomadic Indians), *indios gentiles* (unconverted and settled), and plain *indios* (converted and settled). Frontier societies also had *mulatos*, who were a cross between Whites, in this case, Spaniards, and Blacks. But "mulatos" at times may have been *mestizos*, or Spanish-Indian mixed bloods. There were also a variety of other designations for racially mixed offspring, which were sometimes grouped together under the term *castas* (castes). These designations were all common in colonial society, but they sometimes had different meanings in Borderlands societies.

The formation and nature of frontier communities have received relatively little attention from scholars, and hence our limited understanding of the frontier social structure. For the most part, historians have studied Spain's defense objectives on the northern rim of its vast North American empire. This focus has determined that the area would be treated as a single entity and as a buffer zone, or "Borderlands," a characterization that denied the region—or better still, the settlements within this region—their own reason for being and their own particular evolution.

...earlier focus on the defensive objectives of the empire overlooked the fact that the settlers quickly developed their own goals and were generally more committed to their own interests rather than those of the Crown.

Only within this past decade have these settlements been studied in their own right, and this research has revealed very distinct societies that developed from different expansion processes and social and geographical environments. The first region to be settled, New Mexico, had the attraction of large numbers of settled Indians and thus resembled the core of New Spain more than Texas and California, where natives were organized mostly in nomadic and semi-nomadic groups. The first Spanish settlements in New Mexico were established in the late 1500s, relatively early in the colonial period, and although Spanish expectations there were tempered by a widespread Indian revolt (1680), the character of New Mexican society seems very different from that in the other two areas. The settlement of Texas, which took place in the early 1700s, would have been delayed had the French not shown some interest in the silver mines of northern Mexico. In the middle 1700s other Europeans threatened to occupy the far northwestern corner of the empire, thus occasioning the settlement of California. Large numbers of Indians organized in small groups roamed both Texas and California, and their presence inspired Spaniards to launch extensive mission programs, a factor that would influence the character of Spanish communities there.

Settlers migrating to the frontier encountered diverse situations. For example, they found native societies in different stages of organizational development that facilitated exploitation or made it more difficult. Also, the availability of natural resources significantly determined Spanish-Indian relationships in the new societies. The racial composition of the settlers themselves likewise affected these relationships. By the time the communities were formed in the far northern regions the settlers had undergone an extensive process of *mestizaje*, or racial mixture, and had imbibed attitudes of class and race prevalent in the Mexican heartland. How the expectations for the exploitation of Indians and the use of resources were met or not met, how racial biases changed or hardened depended, however, on various factors, all of which differed from place to place and changed over time. Only by studying the different societies on the frontier can the nature of class and race relationships be understood.

The variety of circumstances over time and place reflects societies that were much more "fluid," or dynamic, than previously thought. The earlier focus on the defensive objectives of the empire overlooked the fact that the settlers quickly developed their own goals and were generally more committed to their own interests rather than those of the Crown. The evolution of these local concerns determined the nature and structure of the various frontier societies. The interplay of all the forces—the environment, the availability of resources, native societies, trade networks, coupled with imperial assistance or restrictions—changed the nature of class and racial status in those communities. An analysis of those forces reveals the principles that determined the character of those very dynamic communities.

REGIONAL DIVERSITY
New Mexico

The settlement of New Mexico stemmed directly from the first thrust of conquest and exploration in North America. The Spaniards' discovery of the new continent had been an accident, a rather fortuitous one, but an accident nonetheless. Furthermore, Spaniards did not expect to find precious metals or encounter fully-organized societies that could be exploited. Once they stumbled upon these societies, they immediately searched the continent for other empires. Exploration took one expedition headed by Pánfilo de Narvaez to Florida in 1528. One mishap after another brought a member of that group, Alvar Núñez Cabeza de Vaca, to Galveston Island on the Texas coast. From there, Cabeza de Vaca headed west and northwest, coming into contact with Indians who told him of the Pueblo societies on the northern reaches of the Rio Grande. The stories he heard were soon woven into a tale of Seven Cities of Gold. Given the previous great findings of a continent, precious metal, and populous empires, the possibility of another Mexico was quite believable.

Eventually, after a cursory preliminary investigation, an expedition was launched in 1540 under the direction of Francisco Vásquez de Coronado, governor of what was then the frontier province of Nueva Galicia. Like other expansion enterprises, this one required a sizeable investment, most of it, but not all, coming from Vásquez de Coronado himself. Other participants also brought supplies, horses, cattle, and of course their personal commitment. The prospect of great returns made it appear worthwhile to everyone involved.

This *entrada*, or expedition, falls in the category of the extraordinary pattern of expansion, in which explorers crossed vast unsettled areas in search of substantial returns. A more common expansionary pattern would have involved the conquest of an adjacent region as population grew and available lands and Indian labor were exhausted. In either instance, the venture was for the most part privately financed by the *adelantado*, the leader of the expedition, who had secured permission for the expansion from the Crown. Usually the Spanish government did not underwrite the expeditions, but it did risk the possibility that, once established, new settlements would require expenditure for defense. Still, the Crown stood to gain from the glory that would come with the expansion of the empire and from a share of precious metals, if these were found.

There were, of course, no Seven Cities of Gold in the northern reaches of the Rio Grande or elsewhere on the frontier. The stories of towns made of gold may have come from an over-eager, very imaginative explorer who saw the sun-basked adobe walls of the Pueblo settlements from a distance. Possibly, too, the myth was created by Indians who wished to send Spanish intruders farther on beyond their own towns. In any case, Vásquez de Coronado and those who accompanied him lost their investments on this venture. But the expedition was not a complete failure. The entrada furnished an accurate assessment of the availability of fertile lands and Indian labor, the more stable, enduring resources for Spanish expansion in the New World.

Hence another venture was launched into New Mexico in 1598. This one was led by Juan de Oñate, whose father headed one of the principal families that opened the rich silver mines in Zacatecas. Not unlike others who became suddenly wealthy, the Oñate family turned to traditional, long-term investments, namely, the *encomienda*, an entitlement of land with an allotment of Indian labor, and to new conquest expeditions. The Oñates were among several contenders for the right to finance the expedition to New Mexico, reflecting how enticing this enterprise appeared. Indeed, returns on this investment were guaranteed for at least three generations. Additionally, titles of nobility in perpetuity would be awarded to those who undertook this venture. When the expedition finally left for New Mexico, Oñate was accompanied by 129 soldiers, some with families, who would also serve as settlers; 83 wagons; and 7,000 head of stock. All told, the expedition would cost Oñate some 400,000 pesos.

An investment of this magnitude was serious business for all involved. The *conquistadores* established Spanish towns in selected areas where there were sparse Indian settlements, but that were sufficiently close to major native populations from which laborers could be recruited. Given the objective of acquiring fertile lands and securing native labor, conflict with Indians was inevitable. From the start, Spaniards claimed the best lands in the area and imposed onerous labor requirements. They were able to do this because they had superiority in arms and horses and at times managed to get the aid of Indian allies in considerable numbers. When the Spaniards encountered serious resistance, as was the case at Acoma, they meted out harsh punishment. The area was pacified, and encomiendas were awarded. Still, because they did not receive the expected return on their investments, the settlers launched a vigorous political attack on Oñate, who had made some serious mistakes in the execution of

the enterprise that may have warranted his resignation. In all likelihood, however, the complaints stemmed from the frustration that the promise of wealth had been greater than the reality.

The only ones in the colonization enterprise who considered their efforts worthwhile were the missionaries. Ten Franciscans, financed by the Crown, had gone along to serve the settlers and convert the Indians in the new lands. The friars' first endeavors were very encouraging. Missionaries tended to attribute their success to their own efforts or at best to the work of the Holy Spirit. In fact, however, Christianity was attractive to the Indians at some superficial level because their culture had analogous ritual traditions and similar mores. In New Mexico this initial "success" of the missionaries actually saved the Spanish occupation of the province.

With the viceroy's backing, the friars then proceeded to take control not only of the Indian spiritual life but of the temporal world as well. In their work the *padres* relied on the assistance of the soldiers and settlers, who in turn were recompensed with allotments of Indian laborers. The settlers, soldiers, and even the governors came to resent their dependence on the missionaries, but they could do little without the friars' help. The governors, who were appointees from outside the colony, were particularly disturbed by this dependence. Soon after their arrival in New Mexico they discovered that they could not wield unrestrained power (usually to appropriate Indian laborers or sell goods at outrageous markups) as they had expected. Conflicts with the friars often escalated into legal action and/or excommunication, and in almost every instance the governors lost because their personal interests threatened to disrupt the missionaries' interests as well as everybody else's. Like all conquests, the spiritual conquest of New Mexico was not carried out simply for the love of God; the conquest involved a contest over power. In order to gain control over the native population, the friars disrupted, with violence when necessary, the relationship between the Indian gods and the people, between the spiritual and temporal chiefs and their subjects, between parents and their children, between the older and younger generations, and between men and women. Only through complete spiritual, social, and psychological disruption could Spaniards control the lives of the natives, who were obliged to take turns providing all kinds of services to the missionaries as well as the settlers.

The early Franciscan reign provided rewards for all, except of course for the Indians. Through the encomienda, the Spaniards required the settled Indians to take turns working for them. Spaniards had the natives construct houses for them, till fields that produced small surpluses, and weave woolen blankets and clothing. The agricultural products and other goods would then be marketed in Chihuahua, from where the settlers obtained other items for themselves and

for trading with the Indians that roamed the plains as far south and east as Texas and Louisiana. Cattle and horses furnished another source of income, but raising stock was riskier since Comanches and other nomadic Indians had perfected the art of raiding. The settled Pueblos were not involved in this last endeavor, but they contributed substantially to everything else.

The conquerors sought to maintain two societies, one Spanish, the other Indian. In the beginning, Hispanics were fewer in number than the natives, but they had a claim on Indian labor that gave them an inducement to remain in this far-flung frontier. Segregation of the Pueblos into a *República de Indios* (the Indian hinterland) as in the Mexican heartland was advocated in order to

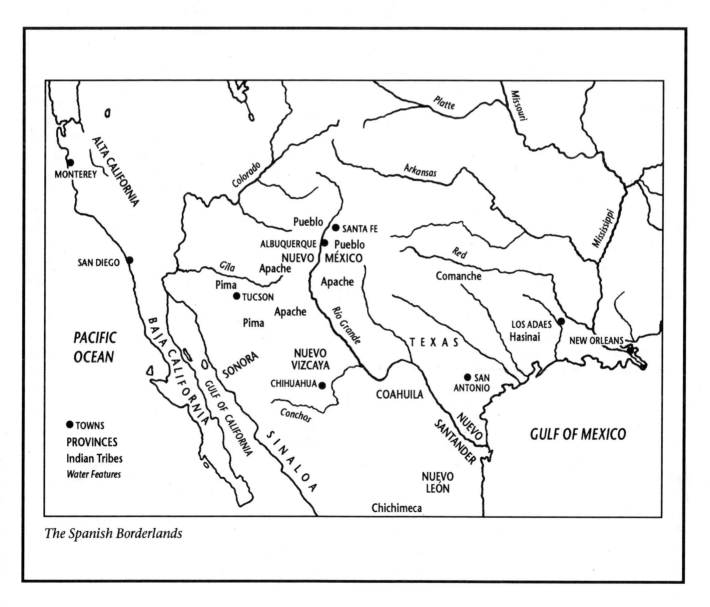

The Spanish Borderlands

reduce the occasion for friction between the two groups. It also facilitated control by limiting Indian knowledge of Spanish weaknesses and reducing the accessibility to Spanish arms. None of these objectives were realized in full, however, and segregation worked to the advantage of the Indians by providing a cover for plots and revolts. Some of these were found out and were quickly put down, but eventually a rebellion succeeded and brought an end to Spanish rule in New Mexico in 1680.

In the reconquest of the province (1692), the Spaniards did not repeat their previous mistakes. The original conquest had by no means been benevolent; the second one was harsher, though in different respects. In the first phase of the initial takeover, the missionaries had functioned only as brokers between Spaniards and Indians, much like the *corregidores* (the distributors of Indian labor) in central Mexico, and as protectors of the Indians. In their quest to displace native beliefs, however, the padres eventually gained full spiritual and physical control of the native population and became the objects of their opprobrium. When the revolt came, the Indians directed most of their anger against the friars, but they expelled all the Spaniards just the same. In the reconquest, the returning settlers did not turn over power to the missionaries.

According to these settlers, their determination to regain the lost province gave them the right and the basis (land) to become the new post-reconquest nobility. Although most of the settlers were mestizo in origin, socially and psychologically they were españoles. Both the old and new settlers who had joined the reconquest effort, however humble their origin, earned the right to receive land and Indians and to designate themselves as "Spaniards." Military officials and retired soldiers also joined the ranks of the españoles, as did other mixed-bloods who emerged as merchants or skilled craftsmen. The old families attempted as best they could to maintain some distinctions between themselves and other Spaniards and tended to marry within their group in order to reserve for themselves the limited resources. But the returning original families were few in number (only fifteen), and

in time their children married the newcomers. Still, while distinctions between the old and new españoles inevitably faded, it remained clear that Spaniards occupied the top rung of New Mexico's ranked society.

The middle ground was held by settled Indians. Despite their conquered status, which required them to provide encomienda services, they maintained certain corporate prerogatives. These rights included a somewhat autonomous local government and communal title to their village lands. Their traditions appeared safer from extermination than before because the missionaries no longer had the intrusive authority they had exercised in the earlier period. But, in fact, Indian culture now underwent greater erosion. The first conquest had been very disruptive, but not overwhelming. The new order, which allowed greater interaction with Spanish settlers, actually brought political and economic pressures on the Indian communities that in many respects resulted in greater change than the interventions of the friars. Movement between the Indian and Spanish societies also brought acculturation and racial mixture, increasingly blurring the racial, social, and cultural lines.

At the bottom of the social hierarchy were the *genízaro* Indians. They had been captured and enslaved in "just wars" of retaliation for attacks on Spanish or Indian settlements. Genízaros could also be obtained through bartering with Indian groups that functioned as brokers with slave raiders. Captured Indian men were often sent south to work in the mines. Women and children were sold to Spanish households as servants. Some of the genízaros were Indians who more or less willfully moved from the edge of the frontier to Spanish towns to escape warring Indian groups. Other genízaros were Pueblos ostracized from their communities for some transactions, some not of their own doing, such as women who had been raped while complying with their encomienda obligations. Marginalized mestizos also came to be called genízaros.

The enslavement of genízaro children ended when they reached maturity, but freedom was often illusive. "Maturity" was a vague qualification. Sometimes it depended on age, which varied;

sometimes on marriage, which could be postponed by the master. Even then, emancipated slaves could become indentured servants. Binding as this type of servitude was, it had more flexibility than traditional slavery, because abuse of the system could be appealed to the authorities. Most damaging was an initial encompassing and lasting definition of genízaros as weak of character, gamblers, liars, cheats, semi-slaves, low-class, without any abilities.

In time some of the genízaros became small farmers, artisans, and craftsmen within New Mexican society. Their status was also affected by other developments. For example, in the late 1700s, when New Mexico faced new, reinvigorated challenges from large warring Indian groups and defensive objectives called for the establishment of buffer settlements, authorities recruited emancipated genízaro families to provide the first line of defense. To entice them to settle on the frontier, the government issued them titles to land grants. With this newfound security, genízaros formed a separate, semi-autonomous society on the rim of empire. There they became farmers and traders between the Spanish and Pueblo settlements and the indios bárbaros beyond the pale of Spanish authority. Genízaros also functioned as soldiers, excelling in bravery and zeal and acquiring honor. In these circumstances, their status changed so that, by the end of the century, being a genízaro became a mark of distinction. When manhandled, a resident of one of these outposts complained that as a genízaro he was unworthy of such treatment.

Other external forces also changed the New Mexican society. The expansion of the American nation westward, first felt in New Mexico with the arrival of fur traders, presented a new opportunity for economic expansion and social mobility. Prior to this time, trade had been directed southward toward Chihuahua, an area that produced many of the same products as New Mexico and competed with it, making goods traded by Nuevo Mexicanos less valuable. As American fur traders and then merchants appeared in the area, certain items, such as horses and cattle, gained over others (cloth, for example) that could be purchased for less than they could be produced locally. Expansion into ranching, in turn, called for a different kind of land distribution and may have produced a new set of elites. The role of the merchants was expanded as they became the brokers between those who introduced American manufactured goods and the silver-rich interior. Even non-elites profited from the new system by turning to cartering. The net effect was the creation

In order to gain control over the native population, the friars disrupted, with violence when necessary, the relationship between the Indian gods and the people, between the spiritual and temporal chiefs and their subjects, between parents and their children, between the older and younger generations, and between men and women.

of a new class of *ricos*, who would rise above the average españoles, and the opening of avenues of ascendancy for the genízaros, Indians, and others at the bottom.

In summary, there are some very clear period characteristics of Borderlands New Mexican society. The first, during the sixteenth-century conquest era, involved polarized Spanish and Indian distinctions. Greater contact between these two groups in the reconquest period, along with the introduction of Indian slaves who could eventually gain emancipation, introduced a middle group that in time would blur earlier distinctions. Defensive goals in the latter part of the seventeenth century and the arrival of advance men from an expanding American economic system also disrupted previously well defined categories. And throughout the Spanish and Mexican periods there were good Indians (the settled ones), bad Indians (*los indios bárbaros* that threatened the settlements), and other Indians, who along with the local mixed-bloods, moved into the towns. The more categories, the more steps for mobility.

Texas

When Alvar Núñez Cabeza de Vaca crossed the area that would become the province of Texas in the early 1500s, he became thoroughly acquainted with the native inhabitants and he reported quite accurately that the area did not meet Spanish expectations. Given the limited technology available to settlers, the land was generally not suitable for agriculture and most of the Indians were semi-nomadic and thus could not be incorporated into the colonial economy. Settlement of this northeast corner of the empire would therefore await the gradual expansion from the heartland northward into Nuevo León and Coahuila. In 1699, more than a century and a half after Cabeza de Vaca's odyssey, Spaniards had established settlements on the Rio Grande, with little incentive to push farther eastward.

A decade before, reports had reached Nuevo León and Coahuila that Frenchmen had landed on the Texas coast with the intent of encroaching into New Spain's far northern silver mining areas. Spanish expeditions sallied forth immediately by sea and by land to halt any intrusion. In the process of ascertaining the extent of the threat, they discovered that the French intrusion had been rather weak and was in fact destroyed by a combination of internal problems and Indian attack. These entradas under Alonso de León were financed by the government and thus formed a particular kind of extraordinary expansion, one motivated by imperial concerns rather than by the presence of the traditional objectives of settlers (land and Indian labor). Such beginnings, coupled with later developments, gave the Texas establishment a defensive character that would, in time, obscure the ordinary evolution of the com-

Economic success and population limitations that opened the possibility of marriage to a Spaniard provided avenues for "passing," that is, changing one's racial/class designation.

munities in the area.

In the process of carrying out the geopolitical objectives, however, Spaniards ventured into the land of the Hasinai along the Neches River. The Franciscans who accompanied the expeditions judged these settled Indians to be good candidates for Christianization and lobbied for the permanent settlement of the area. But the natives proved to be less receptive than anticipated, and the French were nowhere to be found. Without these incentives, the Spanish withdrew to Rio Grande. There, a garrison (*presidio*) and missions spearheaded the advance of settlement. The combination of soldier-settlers and Franciscan-organized Indian towns had functioned as the vanguard of Spanish expansion into the "*La gran chichimeca*," the vast northern lands of the "dog people" (the Aztec name for the troublesome nomads). In this frontier, the missionaries had "reduced" wandering Indian groups into communities resembling the central Mexican villages that facilitated conversion of the Indians as well as their integration into the Spanish economic system. The presidial soldiers provided protection for the missionaries and the new religious-Indian towns and also served as the first settlers in the area. In time, the pacification of the region and the evidence that its resources could be tapped attracted "civilian" (non-religious, non-military) settlers. At the end of the sixteenth century, these civilians had not ventured to the Rio Grande, then the edge of the northeastern frontier.

In the second decade of the 1700s, when the French appeared again on the rim of empire—this time, in Louisiana—the Spaniards lunged forward once again to East Texas. The Indians were as unreceptive as before, but this time defense of the silver-rich north necessitated establishing an outpost near the Louisiana border. To maintain the mission, garrison, and the small civilian settlement at Los Adaes and elsewhere in this northeastern corner, a mid-way station was established on the San Antonio River in 1718. The semi-nomadic Indian groups in that area were prime candidates for missionization, and the settlement's central location proved to be strategically important for the mobilization of troops from the interior to the province and from the San Antonio area to East Texas as well as to the Gulf coast. Immigrants from the Canary Islands, brought to Texas with special incentives, organized the Villa de San Fernando de Béxar, which became the nucleus of a broader community formed by them (the *Isleños*, or Islanders), the soldier-settlers, new immigrants from the interior, refugees from East Texas, and Indians from the missions and from small and large groups that dwelt beyond Spanish control.

The Isleños arrived in 1731, thirteen years after the first settlements had been established, but because the Crown had given them all land-granting authority in order to bring them to the frontier, they quickly took complete control and excluded the *presidiarios* from the irrigable lands. Still, like New Mexico elites, the Spanish Isleños were not able to perpetuate their exclusive rule indefinitely and began marrying mixed-blood presidiarios who had risen in status by climbing the military ranks on the frontier. Isleños also married immigrants who were merchants or were upwardly mobile in other professions. As this process took place and as military and immigrant families acquired land, the prestigious claim to be an Isleño was broadened to being español, despite the clear mixed-blood ancestry of most in the socially and economically ambitious group.

Artisans, craftsmen, and day laborers kept the mestizo, or the more generalized casta designation. In the first half of the eighteenth century, there had been several very precise categories of racial mixture, but their very proliferation may

have created more confusion than clarity and thus the various distinctions were subsumed by mestizo or casta labels. Economic success and population limitations that opened the possibility of marriage to a Spaniard provided avenues for "passing," that is, changing one's racial/class designation.

Two San Antonio case histories exemplify this mobility. In one instance, José Manuel Berbán, a mulato from the presidio at Los Adaes, moved in the 1770s to Béxar, where he worked as a farm/ranch hand. By the nineties Berbán had married into a prominent Canary Island family and listed his racial/class status as mestizo in the 1792 census. Shortly thereafter he was elected to the city council and then became an officer of the town corporation. As such, he felt secure enough to file charges for assault against a member of long-time leading family, and by 1803 Berbán had risen to the status of español. Pedro Huízar, the reputed sculptor of the Rose Window at San José Mission, arrived there in the 1770s from Aguascalientes as a mulato. He did not marry socially upward as Berbán had, but his trade paid him well enough to buy land in the center of San Fernando. Additionally, with his skills he moved into surveying and became an official in the new council of the secularized (ex-mission) town of San José. By 1793 Huízar was listed as español.

There were also locations on the frontier where race/class designations appear not to have been particularly important. The East Texas communities were made up of soldiers, some settlers, and adventurers who lived in Los Adaes or Nacogdoches because they were the meeting places of various economic systems: the Spanish, French, American, and Indian. In this cultural mix, racial distinctions may have been blurred. Much like in the genízaro frontier outposts, where everyone enjoyed greater access to land and where mobility may have depended largely on personal skills or on the good luck of profitable trade deals, in Los Adaes and Nacogdoches clearly defined racial/class lines were not as important as in Béxar. Also, in East Texas Indians functioned more independently than anywhere else on New Spain's frontier.

In San Fernando de Béxar, Indians were at the

bottom of the social and economic scale. Natives found admission into the community through a variety of ways. Some immigrated from central Mexico as artisans or craftsmen. Others were captured slaves that acquired freedom by reaching maturity and became indentured servants or day laborers. Some were Indians who had resided in the mission towns and moved to the civilian town after acquiring some skill or marrying other Indians or mestizos. A good number were natives from small Indian bands who managed to escape missionization and joined the Hispanic community rather than become incorporated into the larger *norteño* (northern) tribes that raided the settlements or traded with them.

Outside the San Fernando community were the residents of five missionary-led Indian towns. The status of the natives there was somewhat analogous to that of the Pueblo Indians in that the mission residents enjoyed certain corporate rights, including communal use of mission lands and herds. Mission resources, however, were closely managed by the friars, as was the government of those towns. Indians were voluntarily and forcefully recruited into the missions from small bands that faced vanishing resources or were pressured by larger Indian groups. Relatively few natives stayed in the missions permanently. Those who did became the middle managers for what appears to have been a rotating labor force. However, this experience at the missions, whether temporary or lengthy (including several generations), provided the Indians the introduction they needed to join the settlements.

Beyond the pale of Spanish settlement were large Indian tribes such as the Apaches, Comanches, and Wichitas. Natives in these groups had become skilled at raiding the cattle and horse herds, for which the Spanish retaliated with sometimes little more than ritual punitive sallies. At times, however, these expeditions were merely covers for slave raiding. In any case, the situation devolved into a pattern of attack and counter-attack that disrupted economic activities of both groups: for the Spaniards, farming and ranching; for the Indians, trading with Europeans and Americans in Louisiana and with Nuevo Mexicanos. Eventually a peaceful coexistence was worked out that brought settlers and Indians in closer contact than ever before, and goods and people moved back and forth between the two quite freely.

The links with Louisiana through the Indians in time encouraged direct trading with that province, despite imperial prohibitions. The trade involved driving horse herds to Louisiana and the importation of manufactured goods and tobacco. These goods, which could be purchased cheaper from Louisiana than through the central Mexican trade network, provided the one avenue beyond subsistence farming for improving one's economic status and was apparently begun by the *presidiarios* who had been excluded from owning irrigable fields in San Fernando. As this trade expanded, some Bexareños rose in status when they took possession of vast ranch lands along the San Antonio River Valley. Others improved their economic condition by providing *vaquero* and artisan services to the new elites. Thus economic expansion paradoxically created new class distinctions while blurring them.

The search for *mesteños*, or wild mustangs, by the settlers undermined mission resources. By the third quarter of the 1700s, the missionary-led Indian towns were on the verge of dramatic change. Recruitment of natives had slowed down and had come to a halt at the same time that residents became more Hispanicized. To meet these changes, the missions first reduced their operations, then shut down altogether. When this happened, long-time Indian residents became property owners as mission lands were allotted. Town dwellers hauled away building stones from mission structures and also received parcels from the surplus institutional holdings. Private ownership did not replicate the prosperity of the missions in their heyday, but that prosperity had been based on the productive, but forced, Indian labor that was no longer available. Also, the market for agricultural products supplied by the mission had evaporated as presidiarios and town dwellers built their own *acequia* (irrigation) system and became as efficient as the missions. As for mission herds, most of these had been driven to the interior, a market not nearly as profitable as Louisiana, which was controlled by the *rancheros* and not by the missionaries.

Thus, in Texas, as in New Mexico, demographic limitations and the broadening of the economic base eroded the early exclusionary tendencies among the Canary Islanders. The new prosperity also attracted immigrants from the interior, more so in Texas than in New Mexico. This occurred because Texas was more closely linked to the Mexican heartland. Additionally, Texas was more attractive because it did not have fully permanent and growing autonomous Indian communities that needed their own resources to survive. Nor did Texas have a surplus of Indian laborers to provide services to other settlers. Given this vacuum, Texas functioned more like a "safety valve" for expansion from the interior than did New Mexico. Immigrants to Texas included mestizos and Indians who contributed to the blurring of distinctions designated locally. In a sense, then, while dividing society, class and race distinctions also provided avenues of mobility and social bonding.

California

Expansion into the semi-arid northwestern corner was slower than to Texas, and indeed would have taken place even later than it did (mid-eighteenth century) had not the area been accessible by sea. This delay was due to the slow colonization of Sonora, Baja California, and other northwestern areas where the indios bárbaros launched a vigorous resistance and occupation came only in spurts as silver was discovered. As in Texas, interest in California displayed by foreigners roused Spanish apprehension and called for an extraordinary leap beyond the unsettled regions. Finally, in 1769, after decades of great expectations, government-financed settlement expeditions landed in Alta California.

The Franciscans, led by the famed Junípero Serra, dominated the early settlements in California for some very good reasons. First, the friars were experienced in the mechanics of establishing missionary-led Indian towns. Second, in California the Franciscans found many native groups that together accounted for thousands of potential recruits. Fortunately for the friars, these Indians were in organizational stages that facilitated their reduction and concentration in towns. Addi-

tionally, there were few sizeable, well-organized Indian tribes to compete with the missionaries. Third, civilian settlement was slow and, therefore, on this front also, competition for Indian labor was minimal for a long time. Thus, despite low birth rates, epidemics, and runaways among the natives, the California missions enjoyed high populations and the friars considerable control.

But mission prosperity and firm control of the Indians discouraged settlement by others and inspired envy and rivalry. The competition came from the few settlers and from upwardly mobile and retired military. Like settlers in New Mexico and in Texas, the first goal of these *pobladores* (settlers) was to find survival and security in agriculture. In the beginning they attempted to wrench control over the natives from the friars in order to get the natives to work the fields. Generally, the settlers failed in this, and they established their farms on their own or with some Indian slave labor. The political attacks against the missionaries continued, however, and even increased as new opportunities for wealth appeared on the horizon.

The opening for the settlers came at the end of the colonial era and the beginning of the Mexican period in the form of trade with the United States. American vessels heading back to New England on their return trip to the Far East stopped in southern California and picked up hides and other livestock products in exchange for a variety of manufactured goods. Ranching quickly became more profitable than ever before, and settlers and missionaries shifted from subsistence farming to cattle raising. With this, a new round of competition with the friars began, this time not only for Indian labor but also for mission lands.

As elsewhere on the frontier, economic expansion changed the earlier rigid structures, this time with the help of an ideological storm that struck with the onset of independence. Liberalism, a philosophy that stressed individual rather than corporate rights, had inspired those who rebelled against the mother country, and quite logically these insurgents also called for the termination of the prerogatives enjoyed by the mission system. On the frontier, the Californios (settlers) took up the cause and demanded that the natives be granted individual rights. They did so not because they were concerned with Indian rights, but because they wanted to reap the fruits of the disintegration of the religious-Indian corporations. The windfall arrived as expected. As the missions yielded to pressures for secularization, Californios expanded their ranch holdings, profited grandly

...by moving up the military ranks through their personal abilities, through valiant action in battle, or sometimes simply through length of service, some soldiers acquired an improved position in the larger society.

from the trade with the United States, and became the new lords of the land. Their elite status appears to have surpassed that of their counterparts elsewhere on the frontier probably because they (the Californios) possessed more resources to exchange for manufactured goods. In the case of New Mexico, settlers there functioned first as middle men for the transfer of Chihuahua silver to American traders and later as livestock providers. In Texas, the rancheros had only mesteños to trade. The Californios, on the other hand, had larger herds and could sell a variety of livestock products. Additionally, they had the assistance of numerous Indians who had quickly become indentured servants. It could be, also, that much more is known about the Californios than about Nuevo Mexicanos and Tejanos because Anglo-American merchants were attracted early on to California in larger numbers and left behind their recollections of pre-1848 society.

Interestingly, the recollections record not the enterprising spunk of the California rancheros but their concerns for social rank. The Americanos never passed up an opportunity to note the ricos' claims to be Spaniards and their ostentatious display of affluence. Most of these observations are transparently, if not overtly, racially biased. But they also reveal a society that prospered very quickly and almost unexpectedly. Only the few

individuals who grasped the new opportunities at the beginning had any access to the new resources. Additionally, the prevalent economic system offered few avenues for expansion, that is, reinvestment, other than those enterprises that produced the new money in the first place. To sum up, only a few gained wealth, they acquired significant amounts of it, and they had little to do with their capital other than to flaunt it. Hence, the seemingly inordinate concern over the display of status.

California, then, appears to have devolved into a society of *ricos y pobres* (rich and poor), with few, if any, stepping stones in between. Shut out by the big rancheros, most soldier-settlers and civilian settlers remained subsistence farmers. Some immigrants from the Mexican interior, attracted by the economic boom in its early stages, found that the promise of prosperity was bigger than the actual opportunity. The mission Indians received some lands upon the secularization of their communities, but, unprepared for private ownership, they lost these lands relatively quickly. Sadly, the natives had by that time also lost their skills for survival in the wild, and there were no large tribes to join as there were in Texas. The Indians then easily became marginalized, often starving, with their numbers reduced significantly by disease and death.

The arrival of more Anglo-Americans changed little. To be sure, they brought with them a more diversified economy, one greatly stimulated by the discovery of gold. But Indians, mixed-bloods, and former Spanish rancheros were all lumped into the Mexican underclass, which increased in size, but worsened in economic condition. The sudden rise to wealth of the Californios apparently had disrupted the full maturation of their communities. Still, other forces, such as family bonds, some incorporation of native peoples, and a regrouping by Hispanics and Indians to meet the Anglo-American onslaught prevented the complete disintegration of the California Mexicano communities. New immigration from Mexico and from Latin America in the American era also reinvigorated those societies.

Arizona

As has been noted, the road to California through Sonora had been very slow. The missionary efforts of the Jesuits with the Yaqui of Sinaloa, below Sonora, began in 1617. But it would be almost a century later, in 1701, that the legendary Father Eusebio Francisco Kino assigned priests to the Pima settlements of Guevavi and Bac in present-day Arizona. By mid-century (1767) missions and *visitas* (unmanned stations or chapels), as well as presidios, dotted the Altar, San Ignacio, Santa Cruz, and San Pedro Rivers and their tributaries in the land of the Pimas. The northern-most outposts were the San Xavier del Bac Mission and the visita at Tucson. The latter received the protection of a garrison with the establishment of the Presidio de Tucson in 1775. While half a dozen or so haciendas, ranches, and mining sites had been established immediately below today's international boundary, above it there were no official civilian settlements. Still, out of a total of some five hundred settlers, some two hundred civilians, probably retired military, artisans, or craftsmen, had joined the padres or the presidiarios on the Arizona frontier.

Understandably, society in this northern region was centered around soldier-settler and missionary-led Indian communities, very much like the California frontier. Racial/class distinctions, with españoles in the top rank, were evident in the center of Sonoran society, but not on the Arizona frontier. Some of the presidial officers came from prominent New World "Spanish" families, but they, like the other soldier-settlers, were of mixed-blood origin. Distinction appeared to have been small since the trials and tribulations of Apache raids created a society more interested in defense, which was secured through self-help, than in status. As in California, the most common conflicts were between the missions and the presidio residents over the use of Indian labor and the little available water.

CONCLUSION

In many respects the structure of frontier society reflected the conditions of the Mexican heartland society. The frontier as a "Borderlands," or buffer zone, which possessed a certain unity and an exaggerated uniqueness, appears more the creation of later historians than of the actual settlers. There were, to be sure, shared characteristics. The four northern-most areas, New Mexico, Texas, California, and Arizona, exhibited some of the same features: defense provided by soldier-settlers, strong missionary efforts, the sparse settlement of non-military, non-religious settlers, and the need to integrate nomadic and semi-nomadic Indians into the Hispanic society. Additionally, in their governance and trade, all the areas were linked southward rather than with one another: New Mexico with Chihuahua, while Texas was bound with Coahuila and Nuevo León, and California and Arizona with Sonora. But the entire north had these characteristics.

Even the shared extraordinary process of expansion through which most of the northern-most regions were settled was not entirely unique to the frontier. With the exception of present-day Arizona, which was part of Sonora, the establishment of the far northern frontier provinces involved a certain "leap" across an unsettled region rather than simply expansion from an area that had become overpopulated. Only after the outposts were planted did the in-between halfway stations sprout. It was as if settlement of the northern middle tiers caught up with, rather than inspired, the advance to the edge of empire. But, then, this pattern is not unique to the Borderlands. Silver strikes in the northern region just above the Mexican core had motivated similar "jumps" across an unsettled region, with the in-between areas filling up gradually afterward.

Defense did play a vital role across the frontier and had a major impact on the nature of communities there because of the presence of soldier-settlers. The presidio provided an important vehicle for social mobility everywhere in the north. Poor, low-ranking mestizo families from the Mexican core and from established northern communities could count on additional income, however little this was, beyond what they reaped through farming to make a living on the frontier. Additionally, by moving up the military ranks through their personal abilities, through valiant action in battle, or sometimes simply through length of service, some soldiers acquired an improved position in the larger society. With better pay, they were able to buy better farm lands or marry "up" in the social structure. These opportunities allowed them to change their status from mestizos to españoles, as was the case in Texas and California. In New Mexico, the need for defense in the late 1700s provided similar mobility not otherwise available for the genízaros. Even non-military settlers, who had immigrated from the interior or who had come of age on the frontier and found few opportunities, often listed their contribution or participation in defense or retaliatory expeditions as actions meriting recompense in the form of land grants from the Crown. Thus, the need for defense on the frontier functioned as a "safety valve" for members of lower classes in the interior, in the northern provinces, and in the Borderlands themselves.

While the military structure offered an avenue for mobility, the civilian structure of the *cabildo* (city council) often functioned as a limitation to social ascendancy. The early settlers in New Mexico and the Canary Islanders in San Antonio used the town council to limit the accessibility to the resources, such as Indian labor and irrigable land, respectively, to lower ranking town dwellers or newcomers. Election to the cabildo was a recognition of rank already attained rather than a stepping stone to higher status. Those who reached this position consolidated their gains and rarely opened them to others.

There were other constraints to advancement on the frontier. The availability of land was limited to Hispanic settlers by the presence of Indians on the frontier. There were the large tribes that effectively checked Spanish expansion through warfare (New Mexico and Texas), and there were settled Indians who needed land for their own survival (New Mexico) and for whom land had been set aside by missionaries (Texas and California). Environmental conditions—the lack of water—also limited how much of this valuable resource was truly available. Further-

more, great distances to markets reduced the profitability of agricultural products.

In sum, the Indians' use of land and the lack of arable land and markets contributed to the small number of immigrants attracted to the area and to the mobility of settlers dependent on farming.

Indian labor made up in part the limitations of the land. But Hispanic settlers invariably complained that they did not have full access to this resource. In New Mexico, where the largest Indian communities existed and where encomienda exploitation was widespread, settlers had to respect the need of the Pueblo population to maintain itself. This limitation created the need to raid nomadic Indian groups for slaves. Lack of access to silver or arable land and the labor of Indians elsewhere in the northern provinces also occasioned slave raiding. But even in this enterprise, settlers competed with the missionaries for Indian labor. The friars usually arrived first and claimed extensive jurisdiction over land and Indians. In keeping with traditional roles they played in the Mexican heartland, the padres became the protectors of the Indians, even as they secured their labors for building the church and mission structures. With their influence with the Crown, the missionaries also limited the extent of slave raiding. Consequently, the settlers did not have the free access to Indian labor they desired.

Trade, however, was the key to social mobility. At first, the far northern location of the border provinces placed the settlers at a considerable disadvantage. Distances to large population centers were great, reducing significantly the possible profits from the sale of agricultural or livestock products. Additionally, distance made goods from the interior very costly. Hence the attraction of the American markets once these appeared on the horizon. In the case of each province the arrival of this very vital economic system preceded the political advance westward of the United States (1836, Texas Independence; 1848, the conclusion of U. S. War with Mexico). Profits from the American trade transformed the social structure by creating new elites, in some instances quite rapidly and dramatically. In California, the potential of wealth and status from the Yankee Clipper trade accentuated the differences between rich and poor. Elsewhere, however, trade seems to have provided new opportunities across the class spectrum.

Despite the developments in the mid-eighteenth and early nineteenth centuries, the economy of the northern provinces suffered some serious limitations. Warlike Indians prevented major expansion, as did the lack of technology in agricultural implements. Additionally, the absence of extensive trade networks meant that fewer goods were available on the frontier, including a variety of food products that would have increased the life span and added to the general productivity. With the population barely able to replace itself and with limited resources, the economy provided few rungs in the social structure. Still, some marginal groups (genízaros in New Mexico, Indians and mestizos in Texas, and mixed-bloods in California) managed some social mobility. Given the limitations, it is in fact surprising that the social structure was not more rigid than it was.

The limited population on the frontier and strong family traditions contributed to blurring the racial and class lines. This occurred because reduced opportunities for marriage encouraged the crossing of social barriers. Españoles, whether by birth or by social rank, intermarried with mestizos and castas who had improved their socioeconomic condition through service in the military or through special skills. Family loyalties then prevented the full expression of the racial bias implied in the creation of racially-based social structure. Furthermore, racial mixture had also taken place in the Mexican core, and the immigration of mestizos to the frontier softened racial divisions.

Religious traditions, such as the *compadrazgo*, the sharing of parenthood through the sponsorship of an infant at baptism or of adults in marriage, also made social and racial divisions less pronounced than they would have been. The celebration of the community feastdays also helped reach out to otherwise marginal groups. On such occasions, as *vecinos* (members of a community), everyone—españoles, indios, mestizos, and castas—shared the same patron saint.

Thus, while social divisions prevailed, clearly their sharpness or dullness was determined by the particular socioeconomic circumstances of each province. In some respects, New Mexico, with a large, fully settled native population, displayed very distinguishable lines between Spanish and Indian, while Texas, California, and Arizona, with sizeable mestizo soldier-settler groups, demonstrate less pronounced divisive structures. But even New Mexico experienced the in-migration of mestizos and the formation of a mixed-blood group, the genízaros.

Certainly, economic growth appears to be the critical factor to social mobility. As the economy began to diversify, even before the formation of trade links with the United States, society on the frontier became more fluid than at the time of the original foundations. Exchanges with the interior and with the native groups that also occupied the frontier provided new opportunities for settlers, regardless of their race or class. So did military service. Society, then, was by no means as structured as it was first depicted by historians.

This dynamism comes as a surprise to many because scholars have not, until recently, examined frontier communities. In the past the historical narrative has focused on geopolitical developments and frontier society has not been deemed worthy of attracting scholarly attention. Lately, however, socioeconomic studies have accorded the frontier communities their rightful importance. What has emerged from this research is a picture of communities where the town dwellers struggled against great odds, most external, though some of their own making, in their economic and social environments, but survived, found security and, like peoples everywhere, dedicated themselves to providing a better life for the next generation.

■

SELECT BIBLIOGRAPHY

Chipman, Donald E. *Spanish Texas, 1519-1821*. Austin: University of Texas Press, 1992.

Gutiérrez, Ramón A. *"When Jesus Came, the Corn Mothers Went Away," Sexuality, Marriage, and Power in Colonial New Mexico 1500-1846*. Stanford: Stanford University Press, 1991.

Hinojosa, Gilberto M. *A Borderlands Town in Transition: Laredo, 1755-1870*. College Station: Texas A & M Press, 1983.

Monroy, Douglas. *Thrown Among Strangers: The Making of Mexican Culture in Frontier California*. Berkeley: University of California Press, 1990.

Officer, James E. *Hispanic Arizona: 1536-1856*. Tucson: University of Arizona Press, 1987.

Poyo, Gerald E. "Canary Islanders, Mexicans, and Indians: The Sociedad de Castas of the Spanish-Texas Frontier." Unpublished Paper.

Poyo, Gerald E. and Gilberto M. Hinojosa. *Tejano Origins in Eighteenth Century San Antonio*. Austin: University of Texas Press, 1991.

de la Teja, Jesus F. "The Structure of Society, The Spanish Borderlands." Unpublished Paper.

Weber, David J. *The Mexican Frontier, 1821-1846: The American Southwest Under Mexico*. Albuquerque: University of New Mexico Press, 1982.

Weber, David J. *The Spanish Frontier in North America*. New Haven: Yale University Press, 1992.

Professor Carla Rahn Phillips of the University of Minnesota is a specialist in Spanish history. Dr. Phillips' research has centered on Spain's economy and society from 1350 to 1750. She is the author of numerous books and articles about the period, including The Worlds of Christopher Columbus *(co-authored with William D. Phillips, 1992),* The Short Life of an Unlucky Spanish Galleon: Los Tres Reyes, 1625-1634 *(1990),* Marginated Groups in Spanish and Portuguese History *(co-edited with William D. Phillips, 1989),* Six Galleons for the King of Spain: Imperial Defense in the Early Seventeenth Century *(1986), and* Ciudad Real, 1500-1750: Growth, Crisis, and Readjustment in the Spanish Economy *(1979).*

The Spanish Maritime Experience

Carla Rahn Phillips

THE year 1992 marked the 500th anniversary of the first voyage of Christopher Columbus across the Atlantic, and the beginning of the Spanish empire in the Western Hemisphere. For over four hundred years, Spain ruled most of South America, Meso-America, islands in the Bahamas and the Caribbean, and a sizeable part of North America, in what later became the southeastern and southwestern United States. Spain also claimed, but did not effectively settle, lands in the middle of the North American continent and as far north as the Pacific Northwest, where Spanish explorers countered rival claims from Russia, England, and France. Spain also had a foothold in the Pacific and in Asia, where the Philippines and other islands formed part of the Spanish empire.

At the peak of the empire in the late eighteenth century, Spanish America alone included about fifteen million people, encompassed in several large governmental units called "viceroyalties." A well-defined bureaucracy and the rule of law held the Spanish empire together administratively. Physically, it was linked by a transportation network over land and sea. This paper discusses the seaborne lifeline of Spain's overseas possessions, but sea transport was only part of a larger imperial system of administration, transportation, and communication, without which the empire could not have functioned. Among the many topics that defined the Spanish maritime experience, I have chosen four: the ships themselves, their crews, common techniques of navigation and marine salvage, and life aboard ship.

SHIPS

Maritime history has attracted distinguished scholars over the years, but not as many as one might expect, given the intrinsic interest of the subject. Moreover, the field is often either overly technical or overly simplified, rather than aiming at a general adult audience. Spanish maritime history, in particular, has not been well studied among scholars writing in English. The result is that we know very little about one of the most inventive periods in maritime history, or about the ships that held the far-flung lands of the Spanish empire together.

There is much disagreement about how the famous ships of Iberian exploration and discovery developed, and how they looked. Few wrecks have been found from the Age of Discovery, and very little research has been done on Spanish ship design. Where documents exist, they often lack the kinds of specific information needed to study design and its evolution, being more concerned with the outfitting and provisioning of vessels in specific fleets. Much of the pictorial evidence we have for ships of the period comes from paintings, illuminated manuscripts and books, town seals, and votary statues, the latter often donated to churches in supplication for a safe voyage.[1] These images can often seem laughably out of scale to the casual observer, with human beings nearly as tall as the mainmast, and features of design schematically presented. Moreover, the illustrations and models are often difficult to identify or date with precision. Given the difficulties of visual evidence, and the scarcity of information from nautical archeology and documents, a wide range of opinion exists about nearly every aspect of the history of ship design.[2]

There is general agreement on a few points, however. During the fourteenth and fifteenth centuries, a blending of characteristics from northern and southern European ships eventually produced the ancestors of nearly all later ocean-going vessels. Mediterranean shipbuilders adopted the northern rig of a square sail on a single mast, as well as a northern-style platform on the mast. They also continued to use ships with a triangular lateen sail, an earlier borrowing from the Islamic world. By the mid-fourteenth century, large ships in various parts of Europe, with a square sail on the mainmast, often added a second, smaller mast with a square sail, or with a lateen sail on Mediterranean ships.[3] Higher permanent castles fore and aft, thought to have originated for warfare, also aided sailors working the lines of the square sails in both northern and southern versions of this ship, which was called by versions of the name "cog." It usually had a straight sternpost, and a stempost that was curved on southern ships and straight on northern ones. By the early fifteenth century a third mast and sail had been added for balance. The southern method of hull construction—beginning with a skeleton of ribs and planking it afterward—came to be used in both north and south for larger ships, although it took centuries for some northern builders to master the technique completely.[4]

The result of this combination of styles was a ship with three masts, the front two (called the foremast and the mainmast) with square sails, and the mizzenmast behind them with a lateen sail. It was steered with a sternpost rudder.[5] With a combination of square and lateen sails and a good steering mechanism, the ship was balanced and maneuverable, able to withstand conditions on the open ocean and to enter and leave ports with some degree of grace and efficiency. From its basic hull design, the ship would develop in several directions, each one suitable for a particular set of needs and circumstances. By the late sixteenth century, every seafaring people in Europe had developed a characteristic set of sailing ships to serve their purposes.

Spain used several kinds of small ships for patrolling coastlines, sending dispatches, and carrying out other support services. The workhorses of Spain's transatlantic fleets were the versatile vessels called *naos*, most often used as merchant ships, and galleons, most often associated with defense or warfare, but also able to carry large loads of people and cargo fairly efficiently. The size of ships in the Indies fleets varied considerably. The dispatch boats were often no more than 50-70 *toneladas*, as small as the smallest two ships that Columbus used on his first voyage across the Atlantic. In modern terms, that would mean ships about 15-17 feet wide at their widest point, and about 55-65 feet long on the lowest planked deck. The *naos* and galleons were several times larger. For example, a medium-sized merchant *nao* in the late sixteenth century might be about 300 *toneladas*, with a maximum width of about 27 feet and a length on the lowest deck of about 86 feet. By comparison, the *Santa María*, the largest ship in Columbus's 1492 fleet was little larger than 100 *toneladas*, which, in the terminology of the time seems to have meant a ship with a maximum width of about 19 feet, and a length on the lowest deck of about 58 feet. (The official Spanish replicas of Columbus's ships made for the Quincentenary seem much too large. The replica of the *Santa María* measures 25.8 feet in maximum width and 86.4 feet in length on the lowest deck.)

The largest ships in Spain's Indies fleets in the sixteenth and seventeenth centuries were rarely larger than 600-700 *toneladas*. One galleon that measured 775 *toneladas* in 1603 was 35 feet wide

Fifteenth-century ship of the same type as Columbus' Santa Maria. *From the* Llibre appelat Consolat de mar. *Barcelona: J. Rosembach, 1518. Photograph courtesy of the James Bell Library, University of Minnesota.*

and 111 feet long.[6] In the sixteenth century, *naos* and galleons had about the same range of tonnages and measurements, but galleons probably had a more low-slung profile and a pronounced forward rake, with the aft castle much higher than the forecastle. Over time the general tendency was for all of the large ships to increase in size and to develop more specialized functions. In the eighteenth century, Spain, like the other maritime powers in Europe, used purpose-built warships that were faster and more maneuverable than the galleons and *naos* of earlier times, but less versatile.

CREWS

The number of people carried on these ships varied according to the purpose of the voyage. An ordinary merchant ship sailing in peacetime might carry a fairly small crew and a sizeable number of civilian passengers; a ship armed for battle, especially if it was a galleon, would carry a larger crew than normal, plus a large contingent of solders and gunners. In general, the number of crew members required simply to sail the ship declined over time, as changes in design made the equipment on board somewhat easier to use. We should remember, however, that crews worked extraordinarily hard in those centuries, managing sails made of heavy canvas and lines made of hemp or other natural fibers. One nautical treatise recommended using 67 pounds of cables and rigging for every *tonelada* of the ship's size. In other words, a ship of 500 *toneladas* would have carried rigging and cables that weighed about 33,500 pounds dry, and a great deal more wet. The basic crew on a ship that size would have been about fifty men, not counting soldiers.

Very few descriptions of the working life aboard ship have come down through the ages. The crew and their officers were generally too busy doing their jobs to have time to write about them, even if they could write. Passengers on merchant ships had considerable time on their hands, but most of them were too seasick or otherwise indisposed to serve as chroniclers of the voyage. To the passengers as well as the soldiers, sailors were a different breed of human being, alien and largely incomprehensible. Cervantes called them

> *heathen and inurbane persons, who know no other language than that used on the ships; in good weather they are diligent; in squalls, they are lazy; and in real tempests, many give orders and few obey them; their God is their sea-chest and their lodging place, and their favorite amusement is to watch the passengers being seasick.[7]*

A wiser and more perceptive observer of the working life of a ship was Eugenio de Salazar, a well-educated bureaucrat born in Madrid in 1530. After he and his family sailed to Santo Domingo on the island of Hispaniola in 1573, he wrote a long letter to a friend back home. Describing the ship's pilot as he gave orders to the sailors, Salazar wrote

> *I have not seen a gentleman as well served nor have I seen knaves who serve as well and so well merit their wages as these sailors. Because if the pilot says, "Hey, you at the prow," you will see them instantly come running to him like so many conjured demons; and their eyes are fixed on him and their mouths hang open awaiting his commands, and he, with great authority, orders them to (do a dozen different and complicated tasks). And when the pilot has provided these orders, it is something to see the diligence and quickness of the sailors in carrying them out, because instantly you will see some on the crossbeam of the topsail; others, climbing by the ratlines on the shrouds; others on the spars; others clinging to the masthead; others with the topmasts; others clamped on and holding the step of the mast to its cap; others grasping the sheets, hauling and tallying the sail; and others clambering and chasing from one place to another by the rigging, some high and others low, so that they seem to be cats chasing through the trees or spirits of those who fell from heaven and remained in the air.[8]*

The varied and extremely heavy work involved in handling the sails and rigging required all possible coordination among the sailors. For this reason Spanish crews, like all other seafarers that we know about, used rhythmic chants as they heaved and hauled on the rigging. Each task had its own rhythm, relating the force of the men to the resistance of the material. One sort of chant had a steady marching beat, used to coordinate the footsteps of sailors walking around and around the capstan or the length of the deck to haul up anchors and do other similar tasks. Another type of chant had a slow, regular rhythm for tasks that involved standing in one place and hauling on lines hand over hand. A third sort of chant used a two-part rhythm, coordinating preparation time and action time, for heavy jobs that required standing in one place and hauling with both arms at once, then getting into position for the next pull. In Spanish, *salomar* meant to sing or chant these various rhythms, and usually one of the crew's supervisors or an old sailor set the rhythm, either making up words as he went along, or chanting what he had heard all his life at sea. The sailors answered in chorus, or kept silent, as the situation required.

An ordinary day at sea had its own steady rhythm for the crew, punctuated by changes in the watch and prayers chanted by young boys called pages, the most junior members of the crew, whose job it was to turn the half-hour sand-clock that kept time at sea. Keeping time as accurately as possible was crucial for plotting the ship's course.

NAVIGATION AND SALVAGE TECHNIQUES

The power of science enabled mariners to locate that most elusive of things—the track of a ship upon the sea. With an astrolabe, a compass, a lodestone, a sand-clock, and a piece of paper for marking the course, a skilled navigator could understand the winds and seas, harnessing the power of nature to serve human ends. Despite the foggiest day, the darkest night, or the fiercest storm, the navigator could calculate where he was and what route he was traveling. Reliable navigation techniques had allayed the fears that had kept countless earlier generations from facing the open sea. It had also opened the door to untold riches in sea-borne commerce, making the science of navigation more profitable than any other, albeit more perilous as well. A ship's pilot could only ensure his own safety and the safety of others on board if he knew his craft.

Part science, part craft, and often called an art, navigation in the sixteenth century still accepted the definitions of the universe propounded by Claudius Ptolemaeus, or Ptolemy, a philosopher who had lived in Hellenistic Egypt during the second century A.D. Both Christian and Islamic science accepted Ptolemy's view of the universe as valid during the Middle Ages, and his reputation was enhanced in the late fifteenth century by numerous editions of the Latin translation of his treatise on astronomy, called the *Almagest*. Ptolemy's geography or *Geographia*, also printed in numerous editions in the early decades of the printing press, added to the fund of knowledge that the European Renaissance inherited from the ancients, describing and mapping the lands and waters of the earth. The Ptolemaic vision of astronomy is often defined simply by its geocentricity—the fact that he placed the earth at the center of the universe—but it was far

"...if the pilot says, 'Hey, you at the prow,' you will see them instantly come running to him like so many conjured demons; and their eyes are fixed on him and their mouths hang open awaiting his commands..."

more than a mere map of the heavens. To Christian scientists, the location of each element in the universe reflected its role in the total system defined by God. In Ptolemy's celestial map the sun, the moon, the planets, the stars, and the heavens themselves revolved around the earth on perfectly formed spheres of transparent crystal.

By the mid-sixteenth century, science and observation had begun to cast doubts on many aspects of the Ptolemaic universe. In 1543, the Polish astronomer Nicolaus Copernicus produced his treatise *On the Revolution of the Heavenly Orbs*. Revolutionary in every sense of the word, Copernicus claimed that the sun, and not the earth, was the center of the observed universe, which modern science knows to be true.[9] Two years later, in 1545, the Spaniard Pedro de Medina published the first practical guide to celestial navigation, the *Arte de navegar*. He did not mention Copernicus, and perhaps was not even aware of his existence, but that is hardly surprising. European scholars took decades to consider Copernicus's startling new notion, and his heliocentric universe was not generally accepted until the seventeenth century. Medina's work was in the mainstream of astronomical understanding for his time, when scholars and mariners added crucial bits of knowledge about the universe that would eventually confirm Copernicus's theory. Medina mentions many ongoing disputes about the heavens and the earth in his *Arte de navegar*, as well as in the other practical manuals he wrote. Such information and the maps they inspired would eventually replace Ptolemy's geography, even as new astronomical information would replace his astronomy. Wrongheaded as the Ptolemaic notions were, however, they could still provide the basis for surprisingly accurate navigation.

Medina described the Ptolemaic universe with extraordinary clarity, discussing the heavens, the stars, the planets, the sun, and the moon, moving steadily inward until he arrived at the fixed immobile earth, the very center of the world that God had created. Each part of his discussion was designed to instruct, and he took great care to tell his readers the sources of the knowledge he imparted. Where scholars had disagreed over the centuries since Ptolemy's time, he mentioned those disagreements, but never in such detail as to risk confusing the mariners for whom his book was written. Medina provided a reason for everything, including why the sky is blue, how the land and water on the face of the earth are arranged, and how the art of navigation was first discovered.

In the more technical part of his manual, Medina introduced the names and qualities of the winds that mariners relied upon to move their ships in the age of sail. He also described in detail the marine charts that pilots consulted to plan their voyages. Each of those charts carried a wind rose or compass rose, as they were called, showing the orientation of the land masses to the thirty-two points or winds of the mariner's compass. The lines emanating from those points, called "rhumb lines," could be used even by fairly inexperienced pilots to plot a course from one known location to another. More sophisticated navigation required a knowledge of the degrees of latitude and longitude defined by the compass, and the gradations between each of the thirty-two main compass points.

The most important parts of Medina's manual dealt with one of the most crucial components of the art of navigation—the determination of a ship's position at sea by calculating its relationship to a point in the heavens. As early as the fifteenth century, mariners had tables showing the position of the noonday sun with relation to the horizon at various times of the year. These so-called declination tables were revised as more accurate observations were made and recorded with instruments designed to scan the heavens. Medina included in a table the figures for solar declination that he considered the most accurate, and modern scholars generally praise his figures. He also included a listing of the moveable feasts in the Christian religious calendar, from 1545 projected forward to 1600. Medina's manual viewed the universe and man's place within it as a divinely created whole; he did not describe the heavens solely to aid in navigation. In addition to discussing the annual cycle of the sun, Medina explained how to calculate latitude in the Northern Hemisphere by measuring the altitude of the North Star, or Polaris, the only star in the nightly stellar procession that seemed to stay in approximately the same place. One short chapter at the end of the book discussed the stars to sight in the Southern Hemisphere, where Polaris is no longer visible.

The method and instruments used were the same, regardless of which heavenly body was being measured. In Medina's time, mariners could use a cross-staff, an astrolabe, or a quadrant. The cross-staff was a simple square-cut wooden staff, about a yard long, with graduated markings and a sliding transom set at right angles to the staff. The end of the staff was held in front of the eye, with the transom pointing up and down. Then the transom was slid along the staff until its upper end matched one point of observation and its lower end matched the other. A typical measurement sighted the sun at the upper end and the horizon at the lower end. The mark where the transom crossed the staff was then converted to degrees and minutes by using a printed table.

The astrolabe and quadrant were more complex instruments, but with the same purpose—to measure the location of a heavenly body in relation to the horizon. In its simplest form, an astrolabe was a flat, circular ring of brass, hollow in the center except for a strip across the diameter, to which was attached a movable pointer called an "alidade." To use the astrolabe, a mariner would hang the instrument from a ship's timber and hold it as steady as possible. Good astrolabes could weigh as much as ten pounds, because their weight helped to keep them steady against the rolling of the ship. The person making the observation would peer through two viewing holes on the alidade, adjusting the bar until the viewing holes aligned with the body he was observing in the heavens. As the bar was moved, it slid along a scale marked on the circular edge of the astrolabe. Once the object was sighted properly, its angle to the horizon could be read from that scale. By the observed angle, a mariner could ascertain the latitude or north-south position of his ship, either by calculating the change from his earlier sightings or by consulting published tables calculated from the observations of others. The procedure was similar with a quadrant, a quarter-circle with a simplified version of the astrolabe's scale. After the quadrant was held or hung up to steady it, the whole apparatus was tilted until its two viewing holes aligned with the observed object. The altitude of that object could then be read at the point where a plumb line crossed a scale marked on the quadrant's lower arc. Typically, the scale would be marked not only by degrees of altitude but also by the names of known places where those altitudes had already been measured.

Each of these processes gave an indication of a ship's latitude, or position north to south. For plotting the ship's longitude, or position east to west, the pilot had to calculate how long, how fast, and in what direction the ship had sailed. The sand-clock gave an indication of how long the ship had maintained a given course. A simple observation of how fast the current moved alongside the ship gave an indication of speed, or the pilot might use what was called a log-line. That was a rope wrapped around a spool and attached to a log or other weight at the other end. The weight was tossed into the water, and the ship's speed was gauged by noting how fast the rope unwound from the spool. This was usually aided by observing a series of evenly spaced knots in the rope, so that the speed was gauged in so many "knots." A Spanish shipwreck off the coast of Newfoundland from the mid-sixteenth century contained such a log-reel, which is the oldest recovered to date from any wreck in the Western Hemisphere.[10]

Direction was ascertained by use of the mariner's compass, arguably the most important instrument of all. In his description of the compass, Medina failed to accept the need to adjust for the compass variation between magnetic north and true north, which many mariners before his time had proven to be necessary. That need was addressed by another early Spanish author on navigation, Martín Cortés, who finished his *Breve compendio de la sphera* in 1545 and published it in 1551.[11] Sixteenth-century mariners throughout Europe found Medina's book so useful that they continued to use it, despite his failure to adjust

for compass variation.

The last sections of Medina's treatise dealt with how the changing positions of the sun related to the phases and positions of the moon, and how both related to the tides that a good mariner needed to know. The *Arte de navegar* was much more than a simple navigation manual. It summed up the whole range of scientific knowledge and practical experience that enabled mariners to understand their universe enough to sail through both familiar and uncharted seas.

Science also informed salvage operations, after the ultimate catastrophe of a shipwreck. Although the vast majority of ships traveling back and forth to Spain's colonies in the Western Hemisphere completed their voyages safely, catastrophes did occur, especially during hurricane season. Most of the disasters happened in shallow coastal waters at one end or the other of the transatlantic passage. Traversing the open ocean was a much safer part of the voyage. Large ships often carried divers (*buzos*) as part of the crew. In case of minor damage to the hull, they went over the side to patch the ship sufficiently to make it to a port for repairs. When a ship suffered extensive damage in shallow water, most, or even all, of its cargo might be salvaged, along with re-usable parts of the hull, rigging, and equipment. With long experience at sea, the Spanish empire had developed a wide range of salvage techniques. One remarkable treatise, written by Pedro de Ledesma in 1623, carefully described and illustrated how sunken ships might be repositioned on the bottom, refloated, or otherwise salvaged, by using divers, auxiliary vessels, cables, chains, grappling irons, and other equipment.[12] Of course, elaborate salvage techniques could only be employed when circumstances permitted, but they helped to make the best of a bad situation, enabling merchants, passengers, and the crown to recoup at least part of their losses after a shipwreck.

LIFE ON BOARD

The prayers of all on board often asked for divine protection against the hazards of the sea. Daily religious rituals played an important part in the rhythm of a voyage. Religious ceremony also provided welcome breaks in the daily routine. On special occasions, quite elaborate religious ceremonies might be arranged, particularly on the leading ships in a fleet. For Holy Week, one of the great solemn festivals of the Christian year, crew and passengers participated in communal prayers and processions around the ship, although Holy Week would have been rather early for most voyages across the Atlantic.[13] After surviving a thirty-six hour hurricane, one ship returning from the Indies in 1622 held a service of contrition dedicated to Our Lady of Carmen, patroness of mariners. Everyone on board attended, with an image of the Virgin, adorned with whatever finery those on board had salvaged from the storm, presiding over the gathering from a portable altar on the poop deck. Death, a frequent enough occurrence on long voyages, also merited solemn ceremonial attention. To honor a senior officer's demise, a farewell artillery salute or commemorative music might be arranged. A character in one of Cervantes's tales saw a black standard on the topmast of a nearby ship, and, coming closer, "heard played on the ship hoarse clarions and trumpets, clear signals either that the general was dead or some other principal person on the ship."[14] Ordinary funeral services were more simple. Unless the ship were very near land, the deceased was usually wrapped in a shroud of ruined sail canvas and slipped into the sea at night, after a brief funeral service, with those on board saying a prayer of "Buen Viaje." As the sailors' refrain went, "The dead belong to the sea, when the land is far away."[15]

With a good voyage, there would not be many such breaks in the normal routine, and boredom would settle around the ship like another kind of shroud. Except for the unwelcome excitement of an unfamiliar sail in the fleet—perhaps pirates looking for a chance to attack—or storms, those on board had to look to themselves for amusement. They might organize choral singing accompanied by guitars, evoking memories of home with popular regional songs; at sea, as on land,

music played an important part in Spanish life. They might present amateur theatricals or dances on deck at night by lantern light. The anticipation of a major religious ceremony could keep boredom at bay for weeks, with crew and passengers alike making their own banners to carry in the processions, using whatever scraps of finery they could spare. Among the more mundane pastimes, we are told, were races among the live animals brought

Having tasted ham and salt pork, the sharks were willing to sample whatever else might come their way, and the terrified sailors could well imagine what would happen if they fell overboard.

on board for food, or cock-fights among the birds ultimately destined for the pot. The sailors often fished when the ship was becalmed, which could often happen in Caribbean waters. Various games also had their following; on many ships, games of chance were not only pastimes, but obsessions, especially among the soldiers and sailors. The latest game from Germany or Rome, the classic games of Catalonia or Burgundy, and every new fad added excitement to the sameness of weeks or months at sea. Civilian passengers on the Indies fleets repeatedly warned their friends and relatives back home not to get involved in the crew's gaming, since many sailors were accomplished cheats, and the play could easily become deadly serious. Some ships' officers tried to prohibit cards and dice altogether, but there was always something to bet on, if you were so inclined.[16] One way or another, the time passed.

In this atmosphere of boredom and dreary routine, enlivened for the crew by hard work, mealtimes came as welcome diversions, even though the quality of the food was seldom up to the standards of land-based passengers. The greatest difficulty was simply keeping the food and drink on board in a wholesome condition. Water was as much a problem as food. A persistent folk idea held that water got "seasick" just as humans did, turning from clear to cloudy and beginning to stink after just a few days at sea—perhaps the result of recently filled casks conditioning themselves.[17] Supposedly the water cleared of its own accord in time, but eventually it went bad, as bacteria had a chance to grow. Nonetheless, there was usually a sufficiency of once-fresh water carried on Indies voyages, even though it became increasingly unpalatable.

Ship's biscuit, the key element of the shipboard diet, resisted spoilage better than ordinary bread, but not entirely. Put on board as close as possible to the actual departure of the fleet, biscuit traveled in sealed boxes or casks to protect it from the damp. Some instructions to ships' masters specified that biscuit storage lockers should even be sheathed in tin, and caulked, lined, and bound with metal.[18] Inevitably, however, the biscuit softened from the humidity on board, and began to ferment and spoil. Eventually a variety of vermin infested it, taking up residence inside the decaying loaves. The crews on Columbus's fourth voyage supposedly ate their meals only after dark, so they could not see what they were eating.[19] Such problems of spoilage affected virtually every ship that sailed, as long as provisions had to be carried for some time. Rats, roaches, grubs, mites, and weevils all contributed to the damage, which increased the longer the biscuit had to last.[20] Indies fleets often carried enough biscuit for the round trip, since it was so scarce and costly in the New World. This meant that some biscuit was fifteen months old at the very least by the time it was consumed. If provisions ran low, the broken bits (called *mazamorra*) left in the storage lockers would be made into a sort of stew, along with whatever else was available, usually water, oil, and garlic.

The fish carried by the armed escort galleons on the Indies run was usually cod, cleaned, split open, and flattened before being dried and salted for preservation. The finished product, stacked and tied in large bundles, kept fairly well, though the humidity and heat in the hold could cause it to spoil as well. Ideally, the cod was supposed to be kept in the open air from about the first of May on, to keep it wholesome longer, but that was not always possible.[21] Hams and salt pork, the former

generally for privileged officers, seem to have been carried in the open air as well at times. On one ill-fated voyage from the Indies in 1622, sharks began following one ship in the Caribbean. Evidently, haunches and slabs of meat hung from the railings of the poop corridors had come within range of the sharks as the ship pitched violently during a storm. Having tasted ham and salt pork, the sharks were willing to sample whatever else might come their way, and the terrified sailors could well imagine what would happen if they fell overboard.[22]

Indies ships usually carried hens in coops on deck, reserved, along with their eggs, for the principal officers and the sick. As the sailor's complaint put it, "To him who doesn't work, a hen; to him who works, a sardine." A more extreme version of the same refrain had the workers eating bread and the non-workers eating salmon and pheasant.[23] Nonetheless, dried cod was the standard fish carried on Atlantic voyages, and salt pork or fatback was the standard meat. At times live sheep, cattle, and pigs might travel on board in addition to hens. In the generally peaceful two decades after 1600, even war galleons habitually carried live animals to enhance the shipboard diet. Like every other living thing on board, the livestock ate biscuit, or at least *mazamorra*. Tortoises appear frequently in the Havana accounts of the guard squadron for the Indies fleets in the 1630s, although the animals may have been slaughtered and their meat dried before the fleet sailed. The sailors evidently stewed the tortoise flesh with garlic, and compared its taste to the finest veal at home.[24]

Wealthy passengers might bring with them much of their own food, or at least supplementary items. Some documents mention passengers who brought lemons, and many undoubtedly carried treats such as honey, figs, oranges, pomegranates, and assorted sweets for the long voyage.[25] Some brought a few hens, if they had permission. For the most part, however, passengers on merchant ships shared in the regular rations provided for the crew, paying the ship's master for their meals.

Interestingly enough, none of the dozens of provisioning accounts I have analyzed, nor any of the descriptions of shipboard life I have seen, mentions how the food was prepared or who prepared it. On some ships, the obvious choice would have been the dispenser. He measured the rations for all food and drink and supervised the pages in setting up for meals, building the cooking fire, cleaning up afterward, and soaking dried provisions overnight for subsequent cooking.[26] It is probable that he also supervised the pages in stewing the dried legumes, salted meat, and fish of the standard ship diet. Nonetheless, there is no proof as to who did the cooking. On some sixteenth-century merchant ships, the master provided paying passengers with water, salt, firewood, and access to a cookstove, where they did their own cooking. The standard cookstove on Spanish ships was the *fogón*, a rectangular metal box, three-sided and open on top, with an enclosed bottom lined with sand. A wood fire was built on the sand, protected from the wind by the three side pieces. Large cauldrons with legs could stand by themselves over the fire; other pots could be suspended by hooks from a bar running from side to side across the width of the stove. One author mentions a group of Dominican monks who brought their own *fogón* aboard, with servants to cook their meals.[27]

On warships, rules for the distribution to each man of his daily rations—seemingly uncooked—raise additional questions. The extreme danger of fire on wooden ships would increase the more fireboxes there were. Regulations repeatedly laid down rules for the use of lanterns, fireboxes, candles, and every other bit of fire on board, for obvious reasons.[28] In the late sixteenth century, the meals undoubtedly were prepared and served communally, because we have detailed descriptions of mealtimes, even if we do not know who did the cooking. By the seventeenth century, it is probable that sailors and soldiers on warships cooked for themselves, pooling their rations with trusted comrades and taking turns tending the pot. Yet the standard Indies galleon of the 1630s carried only two *fogones*, or about one hundred men per stove. It is difficult to know how they can all have cooked and eaten in the course of a day, especially since some of the provisions—salt pork or dried fish and a mixture of rice and legumes—required

long, slow cooking. A law of 1621, which outlawed livestock on warships, also said there should not be as many cookstoves and other comforts on board any longer, suggesting that the ship's standard equipment was customarily augmented by private stoves brought on board.[29] It is clear from the documents surrounding the provisioning of the 1629 Indies fleet that the sailors had to buy some sort of eating equipment, although such items also figured in considerable abundance in the ships' supplies.[30] In the absence of more precise information, we can only guess at what the cooking arrangements might have been. It was obviously more important to specify how the rations were to be distributed equitably than to specify how to cook them.

Mealtimes on board are somewhat less a mystery, though we do not know how many times a day they occurred. If the biscuit ration were distributed first thing in the morning, with the water ration, a few bites of one, and a few sips of the other would have sufficed for breakfast. In the late sixteenth century on merchant ships, there were clearly two main meals, one at midday and one in the evening. The ideal gentleman in Mateo Alemán's *Guzmán de Alfarache* dined on the poop deck, with attentive servants to fill his plate, bringing him "silver serving pieces and more clean drinking vessels than you could imagine." After the meal, they presented him with cunningly carved toothpicks, vying with one another for his favor.[31] The average Indies traveller would have marvelled at a scene of such decorum and cleanliness. As Diego García de Palacio described a typical meal for the crew on a merchant vessel, the dispenser had the pages set up a trestle table lengthwise in the waist of the ship, where all the men could fit who were not on watch. The food was then distributed in communal platters and piles that would each serve four men; wine was poured for them by the pages as they ate.[32]

The captain, master, pilot, and notary ate apart at their own table, no doubt enjoying a somewhat better meal. The passengers all ate at the same time, too, "because in this city it is necessary to cook and eat at the same hour as our neighbors. If not, you find yourself without light and without a ray of love in the stove," eating a cold meal in the dark, as Eugenio de Salazar described the scene.[33] The passengers nicknamed the stove "The Isle of Pots," because there were so many separate things cooking there, and Salazar marvelled at seeing so many meals cooked, so many tables, and so many diners. All talked at meals about the food they would like to be eating instead: white grapes from Guadalajara, berries from Illescas, turnips from Somosierra; escarole, heart of thistle from Medina del Campo—naming what they missed the most. "And you could die of thirst in the middle of the ocean, because they give you water by the ounce, as in a pharmacy, after too much dried beef and salted things, since Lady Sea will not suffer or conserve meat or fish that is not dressed in her salt." Everything else went rotten and stinking, even the water. Salazar complained that you had to lose your sense of taste and smell and vision even to get it down.[34] It is no wonder that only ten days out, some travelers began to dream of the simple pleasures of fresh roasted meat and cool, fresh water from the fountain in their hometowns.[35]

We can sympathize with the complaints of these captive diners. The food obviously offended most of the bodily senses, even at the best of times. Even so, the shipboard diet deserves more attention and more respect than it usually receives. The standard diet for sailors and soldiers on board Spanish ships changed little during the Habsburg centuries. The most important parts of the daily ration were the allotments of biscuit (generally 1.5 pounds per man per day) and wine (half an *azumbre* or about two pints). Together they accounted for the bulk of the calories and much of the cost. When ships loaded supplies on the north coast of Spain, cider might be substituted for some or all of the wine, in which case the daily ration was twice that for wine. The Spanish carried beer only when they provisioned in their Netherlands provinces, rationing it like cider rather than like wine.[36] To the basic allotment of bread and drink was added a standard weekly pattern of food. In the mid-sixteenth century, voyages in European waters usually allowed four meat days each week (Sunday, Monday, Tuesday, and Thursday), with a daily ration of half a pound of salt beef or pork, or one pound of fresh meat, when it was available.

During battles or days with seas too rough to allow cooking, each man received six ounces of cheese, half at the midday meal and half at night. It seems from various accounts that one cheese day per week could be expected in the general meat-day allowance. Three fish days (Wednesday, Friday, and Saturday) rounded out the week, with a ration of either a half pound of dried fish, or six sardines or their equivalent daily. A mixture (*menestra*) of rice and legumes—broad beans, chick peas, peas—accompanied the fish ration, and, in some accounts, it accompanied the meat and cheese rations as well, although it is not clear how the *menestra* might have been eaten on days too rough to light the cooking fires. Three *celemines* (about 14 liters) of *menestra* sufficed for one hundred men, according to an account in 1553.[37] Oil and vinegar also came with the fish ration.

Non-rationed foods, though part of the shipboard diet, do not appear in many accounts at all, whereas in others they are mentioned but not itemized. These included onions and garlic, and fresh fruits and vegetables. One account that gave precise figures allowed a daily average of one-third of an onion and one clove of garlic daily for each person.[38] That same account allowed forty meat days and twenty fish days in the two months of provisions carried, with *menestra* served only on fish days, and beer in place of wine. The food provided for soldiers on land varied little from their diet at sea, although it would have been supplemented by seasonal fresh foods.[39]

Conditions on the Atlantic run followed the same basic diet as that for the European fleets, but with more dried and salted meat and fish than the fresh varieties. The early voyages of Columbus had shown the value of dried and salted provisions, and the list of items carried by Magellan in his voyage around the world provides an extensive catalogue of things that kept well at sea.[40] Most of the ships of the guard squadron for the Indies fleets provisioned exclusively with dried and salted items, along with standard daily rations of 1.5 pounds of biscuit and two pints of wine. The fleet of 1560 allowed half a pound of either salted meat or fish, and 3.8 ounces of *menestra*, in addition to the standard biscuit and wine allotment.[41] Modern descriptions of the treasure fleets written for a general audience are often incorrect on many points dealing with diet, betraying their unfamiliarity with the wealth of archival materials on shipboard provisions.[42]

Official rations on the Indies runs from 1647 to 1651 planned for nineteen meat days in the month, nine fish days, and three cheese days. Later in the seventeenth century, estimated provisions might allow for only one pound of biscuit each day, rather than the standard 1.5 pounds, but it is not clear if this marked a general trend of reduced basic rations or merely indicated unusual years.[43] Unrationed items undoubtedly supplemented official rationed items on Indies fleets as well as European ones. Condiments always accompanied the basic provisions—cinnamon, cloves, mustard, parsley, pepper, and saffron. Onions often figured among the provisions for the Indies fleets in the sixteenth and seventeenth centuries, and the historian Earl Hamilton found garlic listed in all but three of the years he examined between 1503 and 1660, with instructions to the master to see that it lasted the whole voyage.[44] In addition, passengers as well as sailors and soldiers could supplement their diet, if they had the money and the foresight to bring extra provisions on the voyage. Fresh fruits and vegetables would have been likely choices, even though they could not last the whole voyage. Lemons were brought as a preventive against seasickness. In 1577 one recent immigrant to the Indies wrote his nephew in Spain to bring four to six dozen lemons with him should he make the trip, packing them in crocks with layers of sand.[45] The cost of fruits, vegetables, and condiments was negligible compared to the cost of rationed items, particularly in Andalusia, where the Indies fleets provisioned.[46] That may explain why so little attention was paid them in official budgets for the fleets. Unfortunately, most writers have assumed that only the rationed items were carried, and they have analyzed the shipboard diets accordingly. It is wiser to remember that the official rations were often supplemented by unrationed items, even when we cannot know the amount of those items in the daily diets of those on board.

In food energy, the shipboard diet provided amply for Spanish soldiers and sailors in the guard squadrons, with 4,130 calories on meat days, 3,743 on fish days (not counting vinegar), and 3,609 calories on cheese days. The figures for every diet variation rank well above the modern estimated energy needs for a moderately active adult man weighing about 143 pounds. Shipboard diets would even suffice for a very active man, and the sailors on duty in the seventeenth century surely consumed as much energy as the unskilled laborers and forestry workers labeled as very active in the late twentieth century.[47] However unappetizing the shipboard meals may have been, they were undoubtedly much higher in calories than the ordinary diet of the peasantry on land, particularly in poorer areas with an uncertain grain harvest.[48]

Counting vegetable as well as animal protein, any one of the three ship diets I have analyzed far exceeded the standards that the Food and Agriculture Organization of the United Nations proposed in 1974. As recommended daily allowances, rather than minimum allowances needed to avoid deficiency diseases, those standards have been called overly high. Nonetheless, they assure that we are not using a minimal standard nor one that is too high for useful comparison with seventeenth-century data.[49] Without question the shipboard diets got the majority of their energy calories from carbohydrates, but not as large a majority as earlier authors claimed. Using modern nutritional information and caloric equivalents for the major food groups, and figuring a monthly average based on nineteen meat, nine fish, and three cheese days each month, reveals the following rather surprising conclusions. The Spanish shipboard diet had 15.31 percent of its calories in protein, 31.14 percent in fats, and 53.52 percent in carbohydrates, using the standard of four calories per gram for proteins and carbohydrates and nine calories per gram for fats and oils. That was much more balanced than many diets analyzed for the European peasantry, or for oarsmen on Mediterranean galleys.[50] Moreover, it would be quite acceptable by modern standards of good nutrition. In modern analyses, the shipboard diet would be considered high in calories, but the strenuous work done by the sailors required high calories. Had they not been provided by carbohydrates, they would have come from other parts of the diet such as protein, which have more important functions in the body than simply providing energy.[51]

However well-fed Spanish soldiers and sailors might have been on board, they still encountered illness and accident on the Atlantic run. Some of the common shipboard ailments included sea-sickness, constipation, dysentery, and various fevers, and there was always the danger of men and equipment falling from the rigging and of artillery pieces exploding.[52] Surgeons or barber-surgeons commonly traveled with the Spanish galleons of the guard squadrons to the Indies from the end of the sixteenth century on, although Mediterranean galleys and small sailing ships still did without them.[53] In the absence of a proper medical officer, the master's assistant or contramaestre often served instead, giving rise to the mariners' saying that "the ship doctor doesn't know how to cure on land," and that "the hands of the contramaestre are salves for one's pain."[54] Given the state of formal medical knowledge at the time, a talented amateur might have been a perfectly adequate substitute. A ship's surgeon supplied his own medical instruments in the seventeenth century, which could include a sizeable assortment of saws, knives, scissors, pliers, hammers, and probes.[55] The medicines and equipment for preparing them figured as part of the standard equipment of the ship; long before separate medical officers formed part of the crew, Spanish ships carried a full assortment of pharmaceuticals.[56] Surgeons or whoever acted as ships' medical officers, learned to be adept at amputating limbs damaged in accidents or battle, and in treating and binding wounds. Their success rates were probably not impressive, particularly when dealing with ail-

Cures involved restoring the balance of humors that signified good health, and that could often be done by diet as well as by medicines.

ments that were not self-limiting, since the remedies available to them often lacked what we would consider therapeutic value.

Contemporary medical practice, following the ancients, found the source of many ailments in an imbalance of humors in the body. Cures involved restoring the balance of humors that signified good health, and that could often be done by diet as well as by medicines.[57] Spanish ships in the guard squadrons carried a special set of foods for the sick, which in some cases served to supplement the diet of the high officers and gentlemen on board as well. In a typical list of provisions, these special foods (called *dietas*) included white biscuit, sugar, almonds, and raisins, plus eggs, live hens, and sheep, often carried in considerable amounts. Although the "principal persons" on board undoubtedly shared in the rations of fresh meat, it is not clear to what extent they were supposed to share in the other items of *dietas* carried for the "cure and regalement" of the sick, as the phrase often had it.[58] The ordinances of 1633 for Spain's Atlantic fleet called for foods for the sick to be carried in a box with two keys, held by the master and the chaplain. Part of the chaplain's duties included certifying on his word as a priest at the end of a voyage that the *dietas* had been used only for the sick.[59] For the 1629 fleet to the Indies, the *dietas* included 1,500 pounds each of white sugar and almonds, 1,260 pounds of raisins, 6 sheep, 351 hens, and 4,619 eggs, for 3,000 men.[60] Eggs could have been preserved by keeping them in cold seawater during the voyage, as contemporary experts recommended.[61] The live animals would usually come aboard after everything else was loaded, some at Sanlúcar de Barrameda, downriver from Seville, and others in the Canary Islands for the outward voyage, or in Havana for the return voyage.

Where diet, medicines, and the surgeons' skills failed, hospitals took over. Sixteenth-century writers who considered the health and well-being of Spanish mariners urged the creation of hospitals in all major ports in the Indies, as well as in Spanish ports on the north, south, and southeast coasts.[62] Spanish soldiers paid for the cost of their medical care, whether on land or sea. The crown bore the cost for sailors' medical care, and, given the chronic shortages of funds in the treasury in the seventeenth century, mariners' hospitals generally suffered from a lack of equipment and personnel. Nonetheless, they existed. There were at least two mariners' hospitals in Bilbao in 1613.[63] Medical care for mariners on the north coast came under the jurisdiction of an official called the Purveyor of Fleets. One purveyor in the 1620s took a great interest in the welfare of sailors and their families, urging the crown to found a hospital in Santander in 1623, and arguing in general for better hospital care and other benefits for the men in his charge.[64] At about the same time, plans went forward for another hospital in San Sebastián, though it took many years to secure the money to make it permanent.[65] There was still no hospital in Santander in February 1628, when the Atlantic fleet arrived in port with many sick men aboard, after a tour of duty off the French coast. With no hospital, the Admiral of the fleet had to put together makeshift accommodations for his men by requisitioning beds and food from the local inhabitants.[66]

It is difficult to determine the overall death rate among crews and soldiers on the Indies fleets, or among the paying passengers they carried. Some authors have simply asserted that it was "appalling," but without offering any proof.[67] To the developed world of the late twentieth century, the death rates common in Europe as a whole in the sixteenth and seventeenth centuries seem appalling. Illnesses that hardly pose a threat to wealthy societies in the twentieth century were regularly life-threatening and frequently fatal then, to princes as well as paupers. In two

pay books I analyzed from Spanish archives, four out of twenty-eight gunners on one ship died on a round-trip voyage to the Indies in 1634-1635, a death rate of 14.3 percent. That was nearly three times the number of deaths one might expect in the general population of Europe in a similar fifteen-month period, and much higher still than the age-specific death rates for adult males. When we consider the hazards faced by gunners in the guard squadrons for the Indies fleets, their elevated death rate is hardly surprising. Soldiers in one large company on that same fleet in 1634-1635 lost 8 percent of their number to death, about 1.6 times the rate one would expect in the general European population, and much higher than the age-specific rate.[68] Again, considering their occupation and the hazards of sea travel, that is not a surprising figure.

A thorough study of the pay books for sailors and soldiers in the Indies fleets could shed much more light on the matter, but that has not been attempted here. Given the admittedly limited nature of the evidence at hand, the death rates of sailors and soldiers on the Indies fleets seemed to lie somewhere between those of the general European population in normal times and the truly appalling rates that could occur during epidemics or open warfare. Death from disease on land and sea was an enormously greater hazard to soldiers and sailors than deaths in battle, even during the war-ravaged seventeenth century.

All of the topics discussed here—ships and crews capable of withstanding the rigors of oceanic travel, the knowledge of sophisticated navigation and salvage techniques, and the organization and management of life on board ship—made it possible for Spain to send its fleets back and forth across the oceans of the world for as long as the empire lasted. And the Spanish maritime experience was shared, not just by sailors, soldiers, and gunners, but also by hundreds of thousands of civilian men, women, and children who had occasion to travel by sea.

■

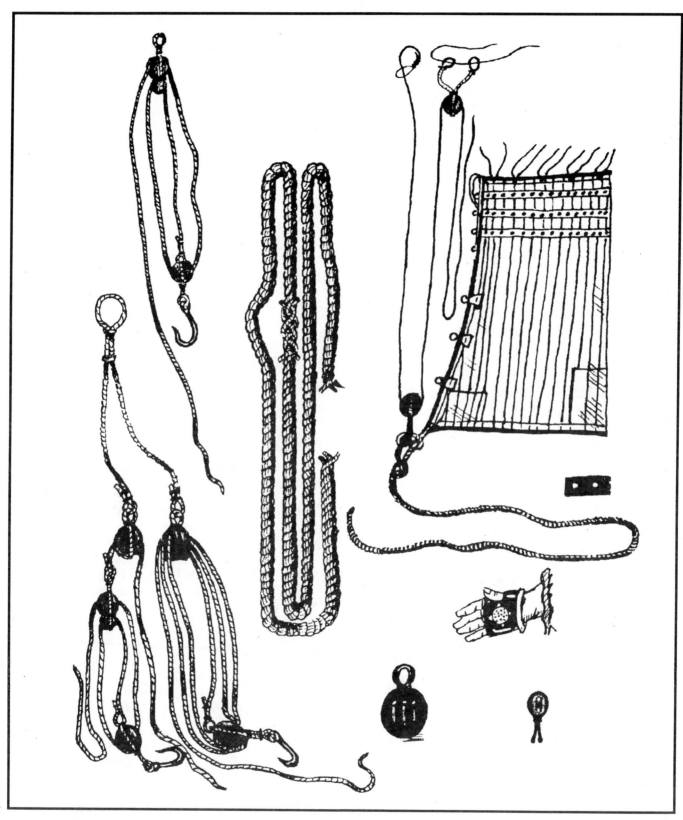

Samples of tackle and rigging from Spanish ships of the period from 1500 to 1750. Clockwise from upper right: part of the main topsail; sailmaker's palm; small block; block with three pulley wheels; spliced mooring cable; two examples of tackle for the mainmast. Representations of the illustrations found in AGM, Marqués de la Victoria, Diccionario *(1756).*

NOTES

Abbreviations used in the notes:

AGI — Archivo General de Indias, Seville

AGM — Archivo General de la Marina, Museo Naval, Madrid

AGS — Archivo General de Simancas, Valladolid

CMC 3a — Contaduría Mayor de Cuentas, third epoch (a section in the AGS)

GA — Guerra Antigua, a section in the AGS

leg. — legajo, or bundle

fol. — folio

ramo — branch, or section of a *legajo*

ENDNOTES

1. See the illustrations in Gervasio de Artiñano y de Galdácano, *La arquitectura naval española (en madera). Bosquejo de sus condiciones, rasgos de su evolución* (Madrid: Oliva de Vilanova, 1920), and in *El buque en la armada española* (hereafter *Buque*) (Madrid: Silex, 1981).

2. See Archibald Lewis and Timothy J. Runyan, *European Naval and Maritime History, 300-1500* (Bloomington: Indiana University Press, 1985), 74-137, for a recent description of this process.

3. Enrique Manera Regueyra, "La marina de Castilla," in *Buque*, 32-33.

4. Richard Unger, *The Ship in the Medieval Economy, 600-1600* (Montreal: McGill-Queen's University Press, 1980), 222-23.

5. G. P. B. Naish, "Ships and Shipbuilding," in *A History of Technology* edited by Charles Singer et al. 3:476-78 (Oxford: Oxford University Press, 1957).

6. AGS, Contaduría Mayor de Cuentas, 3a Epoca, leg. 2214, no. 7.

7. Quoted in Federico Castro y Bravo, *Las naos españolas en la carrera de las Indias. Armadas y flotas en la segunda mitad del siglo XVI* (Madrid: Editorial Voluntad, 1927), 148.

8. Eugenio de Salazar, "Carta escrita al Licenciado Miranda de Ron, 1573," in ed. *Disquisiciones náuticas*, edited by Cesáreo Fernández Duro, 2:183-84.

9. Nicolaus Copernicus, *De revolutionibus orbium coelestium*.

10. Robert Grenier, "Excavating a 400-Year-Old Basque Galleon," *National Geographic* 168(7) (1985): 65.

11. José María López Piñero, *El arte de navegar en la España del Renacimiento* (Barcelona: Editorial Labor, 1979), 187-192.

12. Pedro de Ledesma, *Pesca de perlas y busca de galeones (1623)* (facsimile edition, Madrid: Ministry of Defense, 1985).

13. AGM, Colección Vargas Ponce, XVII, doc. 217, fols. 370-71, contains cost accounts for a shipboard holiday in 1667.

14. Miguel de Cervantes Saavedra, "La española inglesa," *Novelas ejemplares*, 2 vols. (Madrid: Fenicia, 1970), 2:251-5.

15. José M. Gella Iturriaga, ed., *Refranero del mar*, 2 vols. (Madrid: Instituto Histórico de la Marina, 1944), 1:74.

16. Auguste Antoine Thomazi, *Les flottes de l'or. Histoire des galions d'Espagne*, rev. ed. (Paris: Payot, 1956), 192-93; Castro, *Naos españolas*, 150-52. See also Thomas Gage, *The English-American his Travail by Sea and Land ... Or a New Survey of the West Indies* (London, 1648). A new edition is *Travels in the New World*, edited by J. Eric S. Thompson (Norman, OK: University of Oklahoma Press, 1958), 15-38.

17. Cesáreo Fernández Duro, ed., *Disquisiciones náuticas*, 6 vols. (Madrid: Sucesores de Rivadeneyra, 1876-81), 2: 162-3.

18. Fernández Duro, *Disquisiciones náuticas*, 2: 366-67.

19. Gregorio Marañón, "La vida en las galeras en tiempo de Felipe II," *Vida e historia* (Buenos Aires, 1937), 75.

20. Fernández Duro, *Disquisiciones náuticas*, 2:142-43.

21. AGI, Patronato, leg. 260, No. 2, ramo 14. Pedro María González, *Tratado de las enfermedades de la gente de mar* (Madrid: Imprenta Real, 1805), 435-44, discusses how to preserve foods for long voyages.

22. Antonio Vázquez de Espinosa, *Tratado verdadero del viaje y navegación de este año de seiscientos y veinte y dos que hizo la flota de Nueva España y Honduras* (Malaga, 1623); edited by B. Velasco Bayón in *Revista de Indias* 36 (January-June 1976): 305, 320.

23. "A quien no trabaja, una gallina; a quien trabaja, una sardina." Gella, *Refranero*, 1: 8; "Quien trabaja come pan; y quien no trabaja, salmon y faisan." Ibid., 1: 184.

24. In 1621, the crown banned all livestock from the galleons, because they not only fouled the decks but hindered the ship's military exercises. *Recopilación de Leyes de los reynos de las Indias, mandadas imprimir y publicar por el Magestad católica del rey don Carlos II*, 3 vols. (Madrid, 1681; reprint Madrid: Consejo de la Hispanidad, 1943), 3:338. The ban cannot have been very effective, since chickens, at least, appear in nearly every account I have seen for Indies fleets.

25. Vázquez, *Tratado*, 320.

26. Diego García de Palacio, *Instrucción náutica para navegar* (1587) (Madrid: Cultura hispanica, 1944), fols. 115v-116v.

27. Nicolas Louis Scrattish, "New Perspectives on Castilian Migration to the Audiencias of Mexico and Lima, 1540-1580," (Ph.D. dissertation, University of California, San Diego, 1975), 54, citing a document from 1576.

28. *Ordenanzas del buen govierno de la armada del mar océano de 24 de Henero de 1633* (Barcelona,

1678; facsimile edition Madrid: Instituto Histórico de Marina, 1974), fols. 36v-37, 43v. Cooking arrangements and the danger from fire are not as well known as they should be. English ships evidently used large brick stoves deep in the hold, which would have been extraordinarily dangerous in the days of wooden ships.

29. *Recopilación de leyes de Indias*, 3:338.

30. AGS, GA, leg. 3153, letter of 30 May 1629.

31. Quoted in Fernández Duro, *Disquisiciones náuticas*, 2:99-101.

32. García de Palacio, *Instrucción náutica*, 115v-116v.

33. Salazar, in Fernández Duro, *Disquisiciones náuticas*, 2:188-89.

34. Ibid., 2:188-89.

35. Alonso Enríquez de Guzmán, *The Life and Acts of Don Alonso Enríquez de Guzmán, a Knight of Seville, of the Order of Santiago, A. D. 1518 to 1543*, translated by Clements R. Markham, The Hakluyt Society, 1st. ser., vol. 29 (London, 1862), 80-81.

36. AGS, Estado, leg. 513, fol. 165.

37. AGS, GA, leg. 49, fol. 305.

38. AGS, Estado, leg. 513, fols. 165-168, provisions bought in 1555 for the homecoming voyage of Charles I from Flanders.

39. See Nicolás Sánchez-Albornoz, "Gastos y alimentación de un ejército en el siglo XVI según un presupuesto de la época," *Cuadernos de Historia de España* 14 (1950): 165-69, for a comparison of land and sea diets in 1578.

40. See the complete list in Martín Fernández de Navarrete, *Colección de viajes y descubrimientos que hicieron por mar los españoles*, 5 vols. (Madrid: Imprenta Nacional, 1829-59), 4:10-11.

41. Earl Hamilton, "Wages and Subsistence on Spanish Treasure Ships: 1503-1660", *Journal of Political Economy*, (1929): 434.

42. See, for example Robert Marx, *The Treasure Fleets of the Spanish Main* (Cleveland: World Publishing Co., 1968), 38; Mendel Peterson, *The*

Funnel of Gold. The Trials of the Spanish Treasure Fleets ... (Boston-Toronto: Little, Brown, 1975), 85, both of which mention rations that bear little resemblance to information in the documentary sources.

43. AGM, Colección Vargas Ponce, IX, doc. 157, fol. 213; XII, doc. 176, fol. 287; XII, doc. 178, fols. 289-289v. Fernández Duro, *Disquisiciones náuticas*, 2: 134-35 mentions a similar cut in the biscuit ration on galleys in 1678 and 1679.

44. Hamilton, "Wages and Subsistence," 435.

45. Scrattish, "New Perspectives," 115-16.

46. AGS, CMC 3a, leg. 1103-1; AGI, Contadurías, leg. 555, ramos 1 and 2.

47. R. Passmore et al., *Handbook on Human Nutritional Requirements* (Rome: United Nations Food and Agriculture Organization, 1974), 9.

48. Sánchez-Albornoz, "Gastos," 171-72.

49. See the discussion in John K. Evans, "Plebs rustica. The Peasantry of Classical Italy. II. The Peasant Economy," *American Journal of Ancient History 5* (1980): 148. One example of an overly high standard was the one set by the Food and Nutrition Board of the National Academy of Sciences in 1974 for "the maintenance of good nutrition of practically all healthy people in the U.S.A." in the *Sourcebook on Food and Nutrition*, edited by Ioannis S. Scarpa and Helen Chilton Kiefer (Chicago: Marquis Academic Media, 1978), 100.

50. R.J. Bernard, "Peasant Diet in Eighteenth-Century Gévaudan," *European Diet from Pre-Industrial to Modern Times*, edited by Elborg and Robert Forster (New York: Harper Torchbooks, 1975), 37-39; Frank C. Spooner, "Régimes alimentaires d'autrefois: Deux nouveaux cas espagnoles," *Annales: Economies, Sociétés, Civilisations* 17 (1962): 94.

51. Passmore et al., *Human Nutritional Requirements*, 19.

52. González, *Tratado*, 104-327.

53. Marañón, "Vida," 85.

54. Gella, *Refranero*, 1:74.

55. An eighteenth-century collection of instruments is illustrated in AGM, Marques de la Victoria, "Diccionario," fol. 100.

56. AGI, Contadurías, leg. 279, No. 1, medicaments from 1554.

57. Juan Sorapán de Rieros, *Medicina española contenida en proverbios vulgares de nuestra lengua*, edited by Antonio Castillo de Lucas (Madrid: Cosano, 1949), 404-28, discusses the medicinal properties of many ordinary foods and gives recipes of cures for various ailments.

58. Hamilton, "Wages and Subsistence," p. 441, citing AGI, *Contratacion*, 36-3-19/7. The remedies had not changed much by the nineteenth century, although items such as chocolate had been added. Gonzalez, *Tratado*, pp. 362-66.

59. *Ordenanzas... 1633*, fols. 28v-29.

60. AGS, CMC 3a, leg. 1870, No. 3.

61. Sorapán, *Medicina*, 220.

62. "Diálogo entre un vizcaíno y un montañés," (circa 1635) in *Disquisiciones náuticas*, edited by Cesáreo Fernández Duro, 6 vols. (Madrid: Sucesores de Rivadeneyra, 1876-81), 6: 212-218.

63. Estánislao Jaime de Labayru y Goicoechea, *Historia general del Señorío de Vizcaya* (Bilbao: La Gran Enciclopedia Vasca, 1968-72), 5: 65-67.

64. AGM, Colección Vargas Ponce, XX, docs. 146-150, fols. 312-316v.

65. AGS, GA, leg. 3164. The king's representative in San Sebastián was still trying to get funds from the crown in 1635, although a yearly income for the hospital had been donated in 1622

66. AGS, GA, leg. 3152.

67. Hamilton, "Wages and Subsistence," 439.

68. AGI, Consulados, leg. 1040.

Professor Iris Engstrand of the University of San Diego is the author of numerous books and articles about the history of California and New Spain. Her works include Documents for the History of California and the West *(1992),* San Diego: Gateway to the Pacific *(1992),* Serra's San Diego: Father Junipero Serra and California's Beginnings *(1982),* Spanish Scientists in the New World: The Eighteenth Century Expeditions *(1980), and* Old Town San Diego, 1821-1874 *(1976). Dr. Engstrand based the following seminar paper on the journal José Longinos Martínez kept during his visit to California in 1792.*

José Longinos Martínez

FIRST EUROPEAN NATURALIST IN SAN DIEGO

Iris H. W. Engstrand

MONG the noteworthy early arrivals in San Diego, and perhaps one of the least known, is the first Spanish scientific investigator who visited the area in 1792. A small plaque at the Serra Museum commemorates the visit of José Longinos Martínez to California in 1792, but, beyond that token recognition, his role has been little publicized. As a member of the Royal Scientific Expedition to New Spain, Longinos traveled the length of California from Cabo San Lucas to Monterey, recording all that he observed in nature, and giving a first-hand account of Indian life. Although his journal has been published, the recent acquisition of some two thousand scientific illustrations by the Hunt Institute of Botanical Documentation at Carnegie Mellon University has created a flurry of interest in Spain's study of natural history during the late eighteenth century.[1]

Because Longinos was the only person studying fauna in an otherwise botanical expedition, the paintings of birds, fish, butterflies, and animals attributed to the royal expedition resulted from his studies. They represent, in many cases, the first scientific identification and illustration of new species. The majority of paintings were done by Atanásio Echeverria, an extremely talented artist from the Royal Academy of San Carlos in Mexico City.[2]

By the late eighteenth century, as Spain's empire stretched from the tip of South America to Alaska, scientific investigation took its place alongside the age-old pursuit of riches, and intellectuals looked toward the physical and moral improvement of man.[3] Practical inventions and curative plants commanded the attention of scholars at home and abroad. Madrid's newly founded Museum of Natural Science, Royal Academy of Medicine, and Royal Botanical Garden all trained scientists in the tradition of the Royal Society of London, the Paris Academy, the American Philosophical Society, and the major universities of the world.[4] For all, the intellectual climate of rationalism brought about fresh, vigorous inquiry into the known world—the observable fundamentals of natural history.

Preparations for the visit of Spanish scientists to New Spain began during the 1780s. The ministers of Carlos III, king of Spain from 1759 to 1788, formulated plans for two major expeditions that would eventually carry out detailed investigations of California and the Northwest coast in 1791 and 1792. Among the personnel of these expeditions were several naturalists who undertook to survey, identify, and classify according to the Linnaean system all the fauna and flora of Spain's overseas possessions.[5] With them were artists whose scientific illustrations equaled those of other European nations in both number and quality. As the bicentennial of their visits approaches, it is fitting that they be recognized for their unique studies of the natural environment of Mexico, California, and the Pacific Northwest coast.[6]

The Royal Scientific Expedition to New Spain was created by royal decree on October 27, 1786, under the direction of Martín de Sessé, an Aragonese physician living in Cuba. While serving in the Spanish army under Bernardo de Gálvez during the American Revolution, Sessé conceived the idea of a botanical expedition in the Americas. When he learned that Gálvez, his former commander, had been appointed Viceroy of Mexico, he solicited the help of Casimiro Gómez Ortega, Director of the Royal Botanical Garden in Madrid, to aid in his project.[7] By late 1786, Gómez Ortega had secured the necessary financial support from King Carlos III. The royal order called for the establishment of a botanical garden in Mexico City and for scientists to survey, identify, and classify the natural resources of New Spain.

Sessé promised Gómez Ortega that he would make available the Mexican plants that were most valuable for their medicinal properties, especially the Lobelia known in Nahuatl as *tlauchinoli*, "which Dr. Kalm took from the native Indians and gave to the Academy of Stockholm in the year 1782."[8] Additional royal orders called for scientists and artists to "examine, draw and describe methodically the natural products of... New Spain" and to "banish the doubts and uncertainties then existing in medicine, dyeing and other useful arts."[9] Members of the expedition were to collect salaries from the royal treasury for a total period of six years.[10]

The botanical institute established in Mexico City by members of this group hired local artists and trained additional participants for exploratory efforts in the northern regions. In all of its work, the royal expedition was aided by the second Count of Revilla Gigedo, viceroy of New Spain from 1789 to 1794. An enlightened and capable administrator, Revilla Gigedo gave attention to every aspect of the government and progress of his realm. He fully supported scientific studies conducted throughout Mexico and was directly responsible for sending Longinos to California.[11]

José Longinos Martínez was a native of Calahorra on the Ebro River in northern Spain. He had practiced as a surgeon in Madrid before his appointment to the royal expedition as a zoologist and taxidermist. Egotistical and irascible, Longinos came into continual conflict with his colleagues. He frequently differed with Director Sessé on the technical points of museum work, classification of new species, and proper locations for field study. Their discussions finally erupted into an exchange of sarcastic and insulting remarks. Each appealed to the viceroy for the other's removal. Revilla Gigedo finally solved the problem by sending Longinos on a long journey of exploration from Mexico City to San Blas, and from there to California. He instructed Longinos to make a thorough study of fauna and flora, natural resources, mission establishments, Indian life and customs, and anything else of interest in Old and New California.[12]

Longinos reached the west coast of Mexico in May, 1791, and spent approximately two months in the vicinity of Tepic and the port of San Blas; he embarked for Loreto in July. After exploring southward to Cape San Lucas, the naturalist made preparations for an overland journey to Monterey. Despite Longinos' personal shortcomings, and some presumptuous interpretations, his observations of California, which he later incorporated into a journal, contained worthwhile descriptions and interesting comments about California life. Longinos had little patience with certain eating habits of the Lower California natives, which he recorded in detail, but praised their skills in fishing and hunting. He thought the Indians of Upper California showed an improvement in physical appearance over those to the south and seemed more dedicated to useful occupations.[13]

While serving in the Spanish army ... during the American Revolution, Sessé conceived the idea of a botanical expedition in the Americas.

Longinos, after spending approximately one year in Baja California, continued northward to San Diego, which he must have reached some time in mid- to late-July 1792. He described "New California" as a "narrow strip of land extending from the Presidio of San Diego to that of San Francisco; from Lat. 34 to Lat. 39, some 300 leagues [approximately 700 miles]." He commented that the country enjoyed a fine climate and there was little severe cold

because it is all on the coastal plain,

protected on the north by the trend of the mountains. Every year it snows a little, but it never freezes except in the mountains, and only in the highest of them does the snow last for more than a few days. The winter is very rainy, with strong northwest winds, but no thunder or lightning. Rain is rare in summer. From the month of February to June and July fogs are frequent, although in the past few years it has been observed that they are diminishing. The four seasons of the year are very like those of Spain, and all the trees and grains that have been introduced from that country flourish in the same abundance and quality. New California is among the most healthful countries that I have visited. No endemic disease had been noted except syphilis, which makes more rapid progress among the Indians than among the other inhabitants... Its situation, climate, temperature, and other circumstances make this land of California most suitable for the production of grain, fruit, and every kind of cattle. The virgin soil has very few trees and no great variety of plants... Willows, alders, live oaks, oaks, mesquite, etc., are plentiful, as are pines in the mountains and foothills, from which all the missions are well provided with timber and logs. During the past few years grains have been planted at the missions and it has been discovered that, however slight the increase, they have more grain than they know what to do with. If there were a few farmers here of an industrious people like the Catalans, within a few years this land would flourish like no other. I have noted that for the settlement of a country like this it has often been proposed to gather up criminals guilty of grave offenses and other troublesome people, and bring them to these lands, as it were, for punishment. If one considers the matter, however, one sees that such plans are mistaken.[14]

The mission and presidio at San Diego at first "suffered a thousand privations from lack of water, but, since the Catalans came (Hilario Torrent and Juan Mariner) they have had water and such an abundance of everything that they are no longer able to dispose of their grain, livestock, fruit, etc." Longinos believed that all the crops introduced from Spain yielded "in the greatest profusion" and that flax, hemp, tallow, flour, and furs would give the Spaniards a good beginning. After more people came, mines could be opened, and foreigners would be frightened away.[15]

As a naturalist, Longinos studied plant life and listed the medicinal uses for a number of these that he examined in both Baja and Alta California. He was impressed with various species of *Aristolochiae*, known by the name of Indian root, and several varieties of sage. He also described a root that the natives cultivated in the mountains and sold to the soldiers. The Indians said that it would cure any kind of headache by inhalation and any pain in the stomach by chewing it and swallowing the saliva. The root was "very aromatic, narcotic, and resinous, having the property of retaining its fragrance for eight, ten, or more years." One native had carried a piece of it around his neck for many years and even though it had gotten wet "a thousand times" it had not lost its fragrance. Longinos thought it might belong to *Pentandria digina* since it obeyed "the rules of the natural class of true senna, being aperient, resolutive, carminative, etc., so it is not strange that it should have the properties the gentiles ascribe to it."[16]

Longinos observed that mustard was a very common field plant and that its seeds were eaten in pinoles, after being well roasted. They also ate the seeds of the sages, another large seed that they called *silao*, acorns, and pine nuts. He listed the animals as follows:

The most common animals are bears, coyotes, foxes, deer, skunks, raccoons, squirrels, vipers and other kinds of snakes, rabbits, berrendos, etc., etc. Among the

birds the one that is almost a plague in the grain fields is the quail, and recently the thrush (Oriolus) has taken to attacking the grain. [Other birds are] doves, crows, hawks, several kinds of woodpeckers, vultures, geese, albatrosses, pelicans, seagulls, etc., etc.

The animals that attack man are the bear and the viper, the bear especially killing many gentiles. Within a short time I saw two men who had been killed by this ferocious beast. One also sees daily the pitiable effects of viper stings, for the gentiles go naked about the fields. Cattle are attacked by coyotes and by certain of the vipers. Tarantulas are extremely common, but I have observed no ill effects from them, nor do the gentiles fear them.[17]

After passing through the pueblo of Los Angeles, Longinos described the springs of pitch at today's La Brea, noting that animals had been seen to sink in the tar. "After many years their bones come up through the holes, as if petrified."[18] Longinos also explained the ways in which the Indians between San Buenaventura and San Luis Obispo differed from the natives to the south and north. He noted that they lived in communities with a fixed domicile, were attractive and graceful, skillful in gathering seeds, and fond of commerce. In handicrafts, they were talented and resourceful. Longinos was favorably impressed by the Chumash canoes, which were of "singular constructions and extremely light." They were

made of a number of pieces, fashioned without nails or glue, or any tools other than flints but with such precision and neatness that they look like the work of our best master carpenter, with all his tools and rules. Their bows and arrows are different from those of the other nations, excelling them in workmanship, beauty, and effectiveness. They also make war clubs, somewhat curved, and sticks which they use with great skill for hunting rabbits and other small game. Their fishhooks are of shell or bone... They also fish with tridents and harpoons of shell or flint. They hunt sea otters in the same manner as the Indians of Old California.[19]

Longinos challenged the idea that the natives had landed on the Santa Barbara coast from the wreck of some Asiatic ship, but believed that "a Chinese landed, or some person of great skill in his own crafts and other things," and because of this the natives had gained an initial superiority. Because of the lack of trade or even safe travel, Chumash customs had not been passed very far beyond their own borders.[20]

According to Longinos, each of the villages had one or more sweat houses (*temescales*), depending upon the number of inhabitants, which were used by both men and women twice a day.

Like other Spaniards, he thought that the practice of afterwards plunging into a cold pool, streaming with sweat, truly repugnant, especially on days of severe cold. He attributed their lack of hardiness "to this bad practice of theirs... But these people are so addicted to it that the missionary fathers, even in the missions, allow them to have their sweat houses and ponds of cold water for the daily ablutions that they all perform because of their cleanliness and their fondness for soaping themselves at all hours."[21]

The Channel Indians, according to Longinos, were exceedingly addicted to gambling. The game they most frequently played was one in which they concealed a stick in one hand and the opponent had to guess in what hand the stick

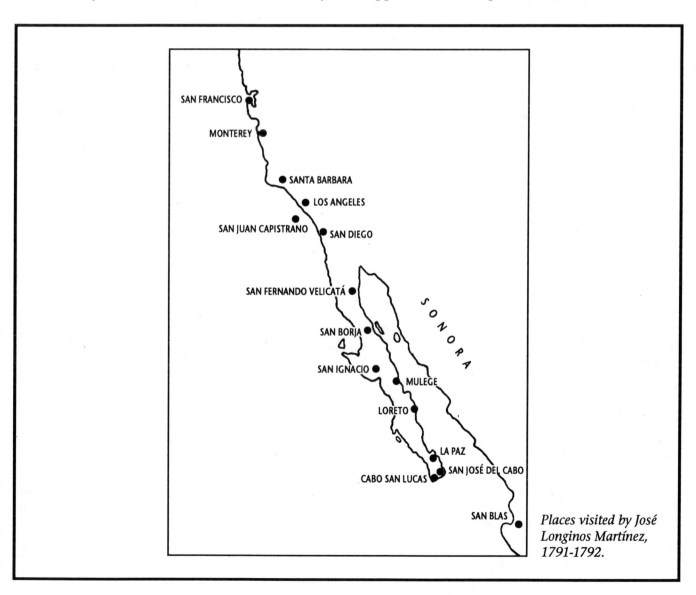

Places visited by José Longinos Martínez, 1791-1792.

was held. In substance, that was all there was to it, but they made "use of a thousand tricks and grimaces" to deceive their opponents and were delighted when their opponents failed, "as if it were owing to their cleverness with their mysteries and pantomimes."[22]

The Indians were also

> *very fond of perpibate, a paste made of the tobacco found in the hills, mixed with ground shells. When fermented this paste has a powerful effect. Shortly after chewing it they become as drunken as if with the strongest liquor. I tested them by giving them brandy and wine, but they liked neither of these beverages [so well]. Dr. Hernandez tells us that the Mexican Indians used to make little balls of tobacco and ground sea shells in order to endure thirst and hunger for a long time; these they placed under their tongue and with the juice sustained themselves, for the little balls made the saliva flow sufficiently to ally their hunger over a considerable period.[23]*

Adultery was not considered a grave offense among certain groups and some of the men even offered their own wives "for any miserable profit." There was also a class of effeminate men, he noted, who performed all the duties of women: "They dress like women; they go out with the women to gather seeds, firewood, etc.; they cannot marry. It is a serious crime for one of them to take a mistress, whether she is single or married."[24] Longinos also reported that the women of the Santa Barbara region had the notion that unless they had an abortion during their first pregnancy, or the baby died immediately, they would not again conceive. "Hence they murder many babies with the efforts they make, the blows they give themselves, and the barbarous medicines they take...so that some of the women die and others are badly injured."[25]

Despite differing customs, Longinos attempted to report his findings without passing judgement. After continuing northward along the coast, Longinos reached the port of Monterey in September 1792. Shortly afterwards he boarded the *Concepcion* bound for San Blas and, during the long journey to Mexico, must have spent time reflecting upon his visit. He reached the coastal port at the end of November but delayed his return to Mexico City for more than a year—until January 1794. Longinos' request for back salary was granted by Revilla Gigedo under the condition that the naturalist submit a report of "all the observations made on the recent Expedition to the Coasts of San Blas, the Peninsula of the Californias, and all other territories... "[26]

This most likely inspired the narrative that Longinos wrote concerning his travels of 1791 and 1792. He rejoined Sessé's group and soon traveled to Guatemala, where he opened a small museum of natural history. Reports about the museum were highly complimentary to Longinos and it appeared that his efforts had finally been expended upon an appreciative audience.[27] Longinos remained in Guatemala for several years making collections, supervising the work of the museum, and giving public lessons in botany. In 1803 he traveled to Campeche in Yucatan and died there of tuberculosis. A letter was later received by the viceroy from Antonio Gonzalez in Guatemala inquiring what should be done with the effects of the "deceased naturalist José Longinos Martínez," which had been left in his care.[28]

The Royal Scientific Expedition received an extension of its original six-year contract and continued in Mexico until 1803, the year in which Sessé and José Mariano Moziño, a Mexican botanist who had joined the Spanish scientists, finally returned to Madrid.[29] They attempted to edit and publish the results of the expedition's extensive travels, but could not get the necessary funding to complete the task. The Napoleonic wars commanded the attention of Carlos IV, and the patronage of natural history was left to a future generation.[30]

If Spain's contributions to science received little fame, it was not because her scientists lacked ideas or failed to record worthwhile observations. The archival volumes of documents, cartographic materials, and thousand of scientific illustrations, plus paintings and sketches of general scenes, offer a record of eighteenth-century American life almost unparalleled by any other nation. Longinos' observations about California's natural resources and Indian life in many instances provide unique and valuable first-hand information. Unfortunately, events on the Iberian peninsula during the early nineteenth century made publication of scientific studies virtually impossible and prevented a con-tinuation of Spain's exploratory efforts in the New World. A number of scholars today, however, have brought new information to light and have succeeded in placing the accomplishments of these unsung Spanish scientists and artists in proper historical perspective.

■

ENDNOTES

1. See Iris H.W. Engstrand, "The Unopened Gift: Spain's Contribution to Science During the Age of Enlightenment," *Terra*, 22 (July/August, 1984): 12-17.

2. Atanásio Echeverría, born in Mexico of Basque parentage about 1770, was a student at the Royal Academy of San Carlos in Mexico when selected for service at the Institute of Botany. The genus *Echeveria*, a succulent rosette plant native to Mexico, has been named for him. See Reid Moran, "Echeveria," *Pacific Discovery*, XX (September/October 1967): 18-23

3. Although the Spanish crown began to further intellectual pursuits early in the century, the greatest impetus for historical and scientific investigation came during the reign of Carlos III. See Pedro Aguado Bleye and Cayetano Alcázar Molina, *Manual de historia de España* (Madrid: Espasa-Calpe, 1964) vol. 3, 370-377; Marcelino Menéndez y Pelayo, *La ciencia española*, 4th ed. 3 vols. (Madrid: 1915-1918); and Richard Herr, *The Eighteenth Century Revolution in Spain* (Princeton: Princeton University Press, 1958).

4. The Royal Academy of Medicine was founded by Joseph Ortega, "first pharmacist of the army," in 1760. During the early 1750s, Ortega had been sent to the capitals of Europe to study the workings of academies of science so

that Spain could follow suit. The Real Gabinete de Historia Natural, which became the Museum of Natural Science, was founded in 1771. The first plants were placed in the Real Jardín Botánico in Madrid in 1777, although the opening date is usually given as 1781. Casimiro Gómez Ortega, Joseph Ortega's nephew, became the director and chief botanist of the botanical garden.

5. The Linnaean system, though somewhat artificially contrived, achieved almost immediate acceptance throughout Europe. Pehr Loefling, who had studied with Linnaeus (Carl von Linne, 1707-1778) in Sweden, promoted his mentor's works in Spain in 1751 and directed a botanical expedition to Venezuela in 1754.

6. Spain's failure to receive proper credit in scientific circles stems from a combination of circumstances. Primarily her investigators lacked the essential ingredient for recognition—the publication and dissemination of new knowledge throughout the world. Even though, in view of recent studies, Spanish scientists were the first to collect and name many species, the several tragedies that befell them upon returning to Spain prevented their continued work. Without proper reporting of their findings, English, French, American, and other scientists achieved the permanent place in nomenclature that rightfully belonged to their Spanish predecessors. See Iris H.W. Engstrand, *Spanish Scientists in the New World: The Eighteenth Century Expeditions* (Seattle: University of Washington Press, 1981) and Arthur Robert Steele, *Flowers for the King: The Expedition of Ruiz and Pavón and the Flora of Peru* (Durham: Duke University Press, 1964), 46-47.

7. Sessé to Gómez Ortega, Havana, 30 January 1785, division 4, legajo 19, Real Jardín Botánico, Madrid.

8. Pehr Kalm, a student of Linnaeus, traveled through North America in 1748-1751, seeking plants adaptable to the Swedish climate. He apparently visited Mexico in 1781-1782 and saw various native lobelias. *Lobelia laxiflora angustifolia* is used in medicine as an emetic, expectorant, vomitive, and antiasthmatic, but is considered dangerous because of its paralyzing effect on the respiratory system.

9. Royal decrees of 27 October 1786, 13 March 1787, and 20 March 1787, Mss. in the archives of the Museo Nacional de Ciencias Naturales, Madrid.

10. Royal decree of 27 October 1786. Describing the sums spent by Sessé's expedition in Mexico, Dr. Samuel Latham Mitchill of Columbia College, in an address to the New York Historical Society in 1813, said: "I wish it were in my power to state the particulars for the improvements of American botany made by the Kings of Spain. There is not perhaps a government upon earth that has expended so much money for the advancement of this branch of natural history as that of the Castilian monarch."

11. See Cayetano Alcázar Molina, *Los virreinatos en el siglo XVIII* (Barcelona: 1945), 92-97, for a description of Revilla Gigedo's government in New Spain.

12. In Historia 527, Archivo General de la Nación, Mexico, D.F., there is an entire file entitled "Disputas entre el director del Jardín Botánico, Don Martín Sessé, y el naturalista, Don José Longinos Martínez," Mexico, 9 January 1791. See also Iris H.W. Engstrand, *Spanish Scientists in the New World: The Eighteenth Century Expeditions* (Seattle: University of Washington Press, 1981), 129-142.

13. Lesley Byrd Simpson, ed. and trans., *Journal of José Longinos Martínez: Notes and Observations of the Naturalist of the Botanical Expedition in Old and New California and the South Coast, 1791-1792* (San Francisco: John Howell Books, 1961), 19ff. The original manuscript is located in the Huntington Library, San Marino, California, where Simpson's first translation was published in 1938. Portions of the journal are also located in the Real Jardín Botánico in Madrid. The Journal will hereinafter be cited as *Longinos Journal*. The declaration of José Longinos Martínez as godfather to an Indian child baptized at Mission San Fernando Velicata, Baja California, by Fr. Jorge Coello, puts him at that mission on 1 July 1792. Libro de Bautismos, St. Albert's College, Oakland, California.

14. *Longinos Journal*, 44. The Catalonians referred to were Fathers Hilario Torrent, who served at San Diego from 1786 to 1798 and Juan Mariner, who served from 1785 to 1800.

15. *Longinos Journal*, 44-45.

16. *Longinos Journal*, 46.

17. *Longinos Journal*.

18. *Longinos Journal*, 49.

19. *Longinos Journal*, 54. See also Campbell Grant, "Chumash: Introduction" and "Eastern Coastal Chumash" in William C. Sturtevant, ed., *Handbook of North American Indians*, Volume 8, *California* edited by Robert F. Heizer (Washington: Smithsonian Institution, 1978): 505-519. Grant has used several descriptive passages from the Longinos journal. A complete guide to Indian sources as of 1975 is found in Robert F. Heizer, Karen M. Nissen, and Edward D. Castillo, *California Indian History: A Classified and Annotated Guide to Source Materials* (Ramona, California: Ballena Press, 1975).

20. *Longinos Journal*, 58.

21. *Longinos Journal*, 52. See also Robert F. Heizer, "The California Indians: Archaeology, Varieties of Culture, Arts of Life," *California Historical Society Quarterly* 41 (March 1962): 1-28.

22. *Longinos Journal*, 55.

23. *Longinos Journal*.

24. *Longinos Journal*, 56.

25. *Longinos Journal*.

26. Revilla Gigedo to Longinos, Mexico, 22 January 1794, Historia 460, Archivo General de la Nacion, Mexico, D.F.

27. John Tate Lanning, *The Eighteenth Century Enlightenment in the University of San Carlos de Guatemala* (Ithaca: Cornell University Press, 1956), 162; Guatemala, legajo no. 704, Archivo General de Indias, Sevilla.

28. Letter of 3 April 1803, Historia 465, Archivo General de la Nación, Mexico, D.F.

29. Moziño, a student at the Institute of Botany established by Sessé's group in Mexico, was a botanist/naturalist who would become best known for his description of Nootka Sound in 1792. See Iris H.W. Engstrand, "Mexico's Pioneer Naturalist and the Spanish Enlightenment," *The Historian*, 53 (Autumn 1990): 17-32; "José Mariano Moziño: Pioneer Mexican Naturalist," *Columbia: The Magazine of Northwest History* (Spring 1991): 16-22; and Iris H. Wilson (Engstrand), translator and editor of José Mariano Moziño, *Noticias de Nutka: An Account of Nootka Sound* (Seattle: University of Washington Press, 1970; second edition, 1991).

30. Sessé worked in Mexico until 1803, when he returned to Spain with some 4,000 plants and 2,000 illustrations of New World fauna and flora. In the fall of 1808, concurrently with the death of Sessé, French forces invaded the Spanish peninsula. Napoleon placed his brother Joseph Bonaparte on the throne that had been abdicated by Carlos IV in favor of his son Fernando VII. Joseph became interested in the expedition's work and appointed Moziño director of the Royal Museum of Natural History. When the French withdrew in 1812, the returning Spanish patriots branded Moziño a traitor and forced him to leave Madrid with his manuscripts and paintings in an old handcart and head for the French border. As a result, the expedition's work became scattered and when Moziño finally received permission to return to Spain, he died in Barcelona in 1820. See Engstrand, "The Unopened Gift: Spain's Contributions to Science during the Age of Enlightenment," 16-17.

Alfred Crosby, professor of history at the University of Texas at Austin, is well known for his books and articles about biological expansion. Ecological Imperialism: The Biological Expansion of Europe, 900-1900 *(1986) was awarded the Ralph Waldo Emerson Prize.* Epidemic and Peace, 1918 *(1976, later reissued as* America's Forgotten Pandemic, the Influenza of 1918*) was awarded the Medical Writers' Association award for best book on a medical subject for laymen. Other books by Dr. Crosby include* The Columbian Exchange: Biological and Cultural Consequences of 1492 *(1972), which has been translated into other languages and reprinted in numerous publications, and* America, Russia, Hemp and Napoleon: American Trade with Russia and the Baltic, 1783-1812 *(1965).*

Native American Crops and European History

THE INFLUENCE OF AMERICA ON EUROPE

Alfred W. Crosby

FRANÇOIS Rabelais, a contemporary of Cortés and Pizarro, mentioned the Canary Islands several times in *Gargantua and Pantagruel*, but ignored North and South America, though Europeans had known of their existence for more than a generation. Few Europeans in the late fifteenth and early sixteenth centuries were aware that Columbus's 1492 voyage had changed history. They were not equipped to think about the unprecedented, that is to say, a previously undreamed-of world. But the influence of the New World on Columbus's home continent was already considerable, and would presently be immeasurably vast. The gold and silver of Mexico and Peru helped to drive an inflation that did more to disrupt Europe's class structure than anything since the Black Death. The discovery that there were gigantic lands stretching from farther north than Norway's most northerly headland to frigid mountains far to the south of Africa's southernmost cape, lands jammed with plants and animals and peoples unmentioned in the Bible, Plato, Aristotle, or Pliny, smashed models of reality that had not been questioned for more than a millennium. "Among the extraordinary though quite natural circumstances of my life," wrote Girolamo Cardano, the mathematician and physician, three quarters of a century after Columbus, "the first and most unusual is that I was born in this century in which the whole world became known..."[1]

Had he known of the ultimate influence of maize and potatoes, humble American crops already growing in European soils, he would have been more impressed with his century. Calories can make as much history as cannon— more in the long run.

For thousands of years we have added nothing of major importance to the domesticated food crops and animals we inherited from our Neolithic predecessors, nothing as important as wheat or rice, cattle or sheep. We have been able to increase the productivity of field and herd, and, more important, we have distributed our Neolithic heritage of plants and animals throughout the world, carrying the sheep of Eurasia to the grasslands of Australia, and the manioc of South America to the hot soils of Uganda. We have shared our crops and livestock, carrying them to lands where their wild ancestors never grew but where they can prosper and so can the humans who grow them.

This sharing has been going on for as long as we have had domesticated plants and animals, but never so extravagantly as in the centuries since 1492. Columbus initiated an exchange of Old and New World domesticates that has had a vast influence on humanity all over the planet, and few places more than in Europe. Europe gained little from the disembarkation of American livestock (the advent of the turkey in the Old

World did not trigger vast changes), but the benefit accruing from the acquisition of Amerindian crop plants has been enormous. That benefit is difficult to measure in total because, to give one example, the nutritional significance of the vitamins of American peppers, a condiment, may well be very important, but condiments are not a bulk item in the diet, and historical records usually deal in tons not grams.

I will concern myself with the influence on Europe of two Amerindian staples, maize and the potato, foods that millions of Europeans have consumed every day of their lives past weaning. These two are well suited to European soils and climates, maize to the south and potatoes to the north, and they are very productive, much more so per unit of land than, for instance, wheat, the standard cereal of European agriculture. Both maize and potatoes can be cultivated efficiently with the simplest of hand tools, and in many areas in soils unsuitable for Old World staples. Maize thrives in sandy soils, and, in its various strains, prospers with ten to two hundred inches of rain a year. Properly dried, it can be stored safely for years; and makes good fodder, in ear and leaf. Potatoes, which in their productivity are to the temperate zones as rice is to the tropics, produce fat tubers in a variety of loams unsuitable for the small grains. Potatoes have the often handy characteristic of growing their edible parts below ground, where they can survive bad weather and—even worse—armies. Both these Amerindian crops produce food faster than wheat and the other staples of Europe. Maize can be eaten green a few months, even weeks, after planting, long before wheat "heads," and potatoes mature in three to four months, long before wheat produces useful amounts of seed.[2]

Let us turn first to the subject of maize in Europe for the good reason that Europeans saw it decades before the potato, and it was first to be brought to Europe and to spread widely there. In 1498 Columbus wrote that "there is now a lot of it in Castile." According to Gonzalo Fernández de Oviedo, writing a generation later, there were already fields of maize near Avila and Madrid. Portuguese and Spanish farmers, at least some of them, were quick to adopt the American grain, and it was firmly established as a field crop in Iberia, particularly in central and northern Portugal and in Galicia in northern Spain, in the sixteenth century. Maize appeared elsewhere in Europe in the same century—for instance, in Spain's Milanese territories as early as 1530—and in North Africa and the Middle East as well, possibly via Muslims fleeing Iberia.[3]

The first strains of maize brought to Europe were probably from the Antilles, where temperatures are not profoundly different from those of Mediterranean Europe, but other conditions are. Europe is entirely outside of the tropics. Indeed, all the chief maize growing areas of Europe are north of the latitude of New York City and Beijing in areas where day lengths vary markedly with the seasons. The first parts of the Americas touched and settled by the Iberians were entirely within the tropics, i.e. in the zone of unvarying day length. It is likely that maize had to undergo a certain amount of adaptation to Mediterranean conditions before it would produce in quantity, and decades must have passed before many farmers found it attractively productive and dependable. Furthermore, I would suggest, the pressure of the population on the land in southern Europe in the sixteenth century was sufficient to force a shift to an exotic food plant only in limited areas.

Before modern times agriculturally and demographically—before 1750, if you would like a benchmark date—the most important limitations on population growth were the Malthusian ones, hunger, pestilence, and war, which enforced "moral restraint." We will concern ourselves with hunger alone. One eighteenth-century estimate had it there had been 10 general famines in the tenth century, 26 in the eleventh, 2 in the twelfth, 4 in the fourteenth, 7 in the fifteenth, 13 in the sixteenth, 11 in the seventeenth, and 16 in the eighteenth, not to mention the much greater number of local or regional famines. We can argue about what constitutes a famine, about how many real famines there were, and about the precise effects of varying degrees of malnutrition,[4] but it does seem clear that poor food or no food discourages marriage and procreation, and encourages a rise in the

death rate. When diet improves in quantity and quality, hungry populations grow.[5]

Traditional peoples are very conservative about food, and when Europeans first came upon maize it looked bizarre on the stalk and in the ear, and tasted alien. To this day the great majority of Europeans think of it as fodder and not as food for humans. But Europeans have often eaten it, even relished it, when the alternatives have been foods of desperation like bark, or nothing at all. The seventeenth century was a century of war, severe outbreaks of plague, economic turmoil, and, on the average, worsening food budgets. Food budgets declined in many areas and population dipped at mid-century, nowhere more noticeably than in Mediterranean Europe.[6]

The crisis of the seventeenth century and, afterward, the pressure of a growing population drove an agricultural revolution of sorts in that and the next century: new tools and techniques, new crop rotations, new systems of land holding that stimulated productivity, and, preceding the other changes, the adoption of new crops. In Iberia maize became a common article in the diet after 1650. In Burgundy and southern France maize entered the crop cycle in the same era, and by 1700 it was growing in every district south of a line from Bordeaux to Alsace, and was the chief food of the poor peasant. In Italy the cultivation of maize rose after the plague and famine of the 1630s. In Piedmont the spread of maize cultivation was one of the sequela of plague and war, disasters that drove a diminished number of farmers to raise food in quantity rapidly. Similar forces pushed maize adoption in the Balkans, but there the early history of maize is obscure.[7]

In the eighteenth century the population of Europe recovered the numbers it had lost in the seventeenth, and rose to levels previously unknown. Spaniards increased from 7.5 million in 1650 to 11.5 million in 1800. Italians, who numbered about 11 million in 1650, jumped to 19 million in 1800. In the same decades the population of England and Wales leaped from 5 million to 9.25 million; that of France from 16 million to 29 million; and so on.[8] More Europeans needed food than ever before, and the land owners and merchants, fixated on the profits to be made in the markets of the growing cities, drove the peasants to produce cash crops, and to restrict themselves to smaller plots per capita from which to produce their own rough fare. The effect was the cultivation of more and more land, greater efficiency, and—in southern Europe—the spread of maize. In the backward southwest of France, where wheat returned five grains for every one sown, maize prospered in the early rains and hot summers, and returned twenty-five and even one hundred. In parts of Languedoc maize reduced the fallow year from one in two to one in three. In northern Italy maize production darted forward, and in time exceeded wheat, rye, and the other anciently familiar grains in Lombardy. In the mid-eighteenth century Tobias Smollett, touring France and Italy, wrote that the nourishment of the poor peasants consisted "of a kind of meal called Polenta, made of Indian corn, which is very nourishing and agreeable." Even where the people could afford food of higher prestige, they valued maize as fodder, both the ears and the leaves. In the expanse of central and eastern Europe drained by the Danube, maize appeared as an important crop in the years around 1700, and became a vital one by the end of the century. By 1800 the peasants of southern Russia were raising this Amerindian crop as well. Its history in the Balkans still under Ottoman rule is not as well known, but we do know that it was raised there in quantity in the eighteenth century. By the nineteenth century what North Americans call corn meal mush was a common item of peasant diet, in wide areas

In 1662 the Royal Society, prompted by no less than Robert Boyle, writing from his Irish estate, recommended the potato as insurance against famine.

the staple, from Galicia to Bessarabia under a variety of names: *millasse, polenta, mamaliga,* and others.[9]

In the nineteenth century the population surge of Europe accelerated into a population explosion—Iberia, Italy, and the Balkans rose from just over 40 million in 1800 to just short of 50 million by 1850, and to 70 million in 1900. For at least the first half of the century the expansion of maize cultivation and of the number of Mediterranean, Danubian, and Balkan peasants who utilized it as their staple continued to rise.[10] That is only more of what we have already covered. The time has come to turn north. In southern Europe maize was regionally important west of the Adriatic, and of major national importance to the east, as in Hungary and Rumania. In the north the potato was of major importance everywhere.

The European saga of the potato lagged behind that of maize. The potato was not a Caribbean or Mexican crop, and the first European probably did not see it until Pizarro's invasion of the Incan Empire in the early 1530s. It seems that it was not brought to Spain for another forty years, the explanation for the lack of Spanish interest in it perhaps being that it was not only very different from their current staples, but a cool weather plant unsuitable for Mediterranean Europe except for the high country. The northern Europeans, whose climate was suited to the potato, lagged many decades behind the Iberians in their contacts with America.

The northerners were in need of something with the qualities of the American potato because they were still dependent on the crops developed during the Neolithic in the Middle East, particularly wheat, barley, rye, and oats. The last three did better in the higher latitudes than wheat, but none of the four were as productive or as dependable as the northerners needed to support population expansion or advances in the complexity and richness of their cultures. Wheat, the classic food of the ancient Mediterranean world, was really at its northern extreme in the lands washed by the English Channel, North Sea, and Baltic.[11] (London, Amsterdam, and Berlin are approximately on a line with southern Siberia and the tip of Kamchatka, with which they share the white nights of summer and the brief days of winter). Early frost, late spring, a gloomy summer, and hunger would follow. In addition, the small grains, notably rye, were liable to molds and fungus in the cool, wet weather, and those who ate them to ergotism and other disorders—perhaps in greater numbers than we imagine.[12] Irish, Britons, Normans, Netherlanders, Scandinavians, North Germans, Poles, and Russians were in need of a very productive crop that would thrive free of parasites in the northern latitudes and climates.

The answer to their needs, the American white potato, was a long time in coming to Europe, and once ashore, about 1570, it attracted little interest. It showed up in Belgium in 1587 and in Vienna in the following year, where it was apparently regarded as little more than a garden novelty.[13] Europeans were slow to adopt the potato for several reasons. It was, by the standards of their agriculture and cookery, bizarre and possibly dangerous. Furthermore, it is likely that the first potatoes brought to Europe were unsuited to the latitudes of northern Europe. These plants were probably collected in the mountain valleys and plateaus of Peru, where the temperatures are cool not because of the latitude but because of the altitude. The lands central to the Incan Empire lay in the tropics, where days are of similar length throughout the year. Peruvian potatoes blossom, produce seed and tubers without signals from the changing day lengths of late summer and autumn. These plants react to the long days of European summers by growing and growing, producing tier after tier of flowers, and when the growing season ends have produced only small potatoes, if any at all. Eventually, European farmers obtained potato plants from Chile adapted to fluctuating day lengths like those of northern Europe, but that seems not to have happened until the last half of the 1800s, a century after the potato became a staple for such as the Irish, Scottish, Flemish, and Palatinate peasants.[14]

The adaptation of the Peruvian potato plant to European conditions must have taken place in the seventeenth or eighteenth centuries, but there is no documentation on the matter. Simple farmers, selecting seeds for yield and early maturity of tubers, developed the plant that would revolutionize northern agriculture. (They must have planted the seeds and not pieces of the potatoes containing "eyes," as is usually the practice with this crop, because that is cloning, and would have produced generation after generation of the same tropical plants). In Viverais in the Rhone Alps, for instance, where the population grew faster than cereal production, the peasants improvised their own humble agricultural revolution in the eighteenth century, utilizing as new food sources the chestnut and their own version of the *truffe blanche* or *pomme de terre*—the white potato.[15]

The Irish people provided a greater and more influential example, the classic example of the effect of the potato on a European population. Ireland's seventeenth century crisis—the Cromwellian invasion, famine, mass evictions, and the throttling of the export trade—forced the peasantry and the native aristocracy, reduced to peasant status, to seek means to extract the greatest amount of nourishment as safely and swiftly as possible from the least amount of land, and that often land of marginal quality. They discovered that an acre and a half would provide enough potatoes for a family of five, as compared to five acres needed to produce the equivalent in grain; and furthermore, discovered that they only needed a spade to plant, tend, and harvest the crop. An adult could survive and be healthy on five or so kilograms of potatoes a day and a bit of milk.[16] In 1662 the Royal Society, prompted by no less than Robert Boyle, writing from his Irish estate, recommended the potato as insurance against famine.[17]

Food shortages in the Rhineland and Flanders during the wars of Louis XIV, and harvest failures in Germany in 1740 and 1770-1772 convinced many there of the value of the potato. French soldiers returning from imprisonment in Germany during the Seven Years' War brought the news home, and the potato began its sweep across northern France. Poor grain harvests and rising food prices in the last third of the century accelerated the adoption of the potato everywhere on the Continent suited to the tuber. Royalty and governments—Frederick the Great, Louis XVI, France's Committee of Public Safety—urged the cultivation of the crop. By the end of the eighteenth century wherever in northwest Europe the peasants' land holdings were small and getting smaller, as dense populations became denser, and wherever landlords were obliging tenants to raise food for local consumption on smaller plots so as to free land for cash crops, the potato spread. In Ireland, parts of Scotland and the north of England, Flanders, the Rhineland, southwestern Germany, and Switzerland the potato became the peasant staple. In Brandenberg, to cite another example, sowings of potatoes rose from 1,653 *wispel* (a measure of about 24 bushels each) in the year 1765 to 21,188 in 1801.[18] At the beginning of the new century, in the midst of the Napoleonic Wars, an extended crisis that also spurred the cultivation of potatoes, Alexander von Humboldt announced the obvious: the tuber was already indispensable for a large portion of the peoples of northern Europe.[19]

In the nineteenth century the potato became more nearly indispensable in the European diet than ever before or since, with the exception of the years of two world wars of the succeeding century. In no other country was the dependence on the tuber so nearly total as in Ireland, but in every major northern state cultivation of the potato climbed to unprecedented levels. In 1841 France, one of the major producers, harvested 177 million hectoliters of potatoes. In Sweden production of the tubers increased six times over from 1800-1810 to 1820-1830. In Prussia the area devoted to potatoes increased ten-fold between 1816 and 1861, and in the nation of Germany that grew up around the Prussian core the area under potatoes grew 66 per cent between 1850 and 1882.[20] In Russia, where Catherine the Great's attempt to stimulate potato cultivation after the famine of 1765 had come to little, crop failures in 1838-1839 turned the trick and in the last half of the century potato production went up more than 400 percent.[21]

The years around 1900 mark the peak of the importance of the potato in European history. In the period 1910-1914 the annual consumption of potatoes per capita in the United Kingdom was 97 kilograms, 176 in France, 199 in Germany, 206.5 in Belgium. Even Italians, for all their fields of maize, accounted for 27.8 kilograms each.[22]

Ironically, the advent of two crops that allowed large numbers of poor to live on the productivity of small pieces of land did not necessarily improve their lot. The other side of the coin of hearty meals was disease and starvation. The acquisition of a new and richly productive crop could perpetuate inefficient systems of agriculture and of exploitive class relationships. In Ireland the productivity of the potato made it possible for landlords to evict the peasantry from vast areas, where livestock and grains for the English market and cash were produced. In southwest France the story was much the same, but there maize was the crop that made it possible for peasants to survive using primitive methods on less land than they had ever needed for the purpose before.[23]

Essential to this exploitation of the peasantry was the reduction of the diets of many peasants to one staple, with all the dangers that entails. Maize provides good nourishment calorically, and in other ways as well, but is far from a perfect food, being deficient in the vitamin B complex constituents, especially niacin. It will serve well for the bulk of a diet, but must be supplemented with foods, meats and greens, that contain what it lacks. In 1755 an article appeared in a French medical journal on a strange malady then endemic in Asturias, where the lower classes were heavily dependent on maize. The symptoms were redness of and even crusting of the skin, and in the worst cases feebleness, tremors, depression, mania, and even death. The Italian word for it was *pellagra*, a word in some local dialect meaning rough skin. In 1808 a Professor Bunira reported that he had (doubtlessly in emulation of Dr. Edward Jenner's work with smallpox) collected fluid from the sores of pellagra victims and used it to inoculate animals and even himself, but with no pellagrous result. Without understanding of the cause of pellagra, there was no possibility of controlling the disease. It continued to appear in the provinces of earliest dependence on maize in Iberia, France, and Italy, and was soon reported in the Balkans, southern Russia (and, in time, in the United States, Latin America, Egypt, and South Africa). In 1830 there were 20,282 cases of pellagra in Lombardy, or 1.4 percent of the entire population. In 1856 the number had risen to 37,628 cases, or 1.5 percent of the population. In the second and third decades of the twentieth century Dr. Joseph Goldberger of the United States discovered that pellagra was not a disease of infection but one of malnutrition, and that its cause was unvarying maize diet. That discovery and a rising standard of living enabled North Americans and Europeans to control and cure the disease, and by mid-century pellagra was almost unknown in their parts of the globe (though not from the Third World, where it still ravages the very poor). In the previous two centuries hundreds of thousands had died of the disease, and an uncounted number, no doubt millions, had been ravaged by its symptoms. And this all because maize was so wondrous a food that the populations of entire provinces slipped into nearly absolute dependence upon it.[24]

A diet of potatoes, with very few inexpensive supplements, will support not only survival, but health. In 1776 Adam Smith praised the potato as healthy food, remarking that[25]

> The chairmen, porters, and coal-heavers in London, and those unfortunate women who live by prostitution, the strongest men and the most beautiful women perhaps in the British dominions, are said to be, the greater part of them, from the lowest rank of people in Ireland, who are generally fed with this root. No food can afford a more decisive proof of its nourishing quality, or of its being peculiarly suitable to the health of the human constitution.

But he also noted that potatoes were not a perfect food in all ways: they tended to rot, and it was impractical to store one year's crop for consumption in another year. Furthermore, he pointed out that if their only or chief effect on their consumers was to enable them to multiply, then the end result would be a rise in land rents and not an improvement in the consumers' lot. His intellectual heir, David Ricardo, wrote to an Anglo-Irish friend in 1822 that the Irish dependence on potatoes worried him. "I think we are not only richer and happier in England than in Ireland and…are never so near actual famine than you are…" He asked, "What can you put in the scale against this dreadful evil?" The three million Irish of 1750 grew to 5.25 million in 1800, and surged to an all-time peak of over eight million in 1841. Disraeli declared Ireland the most densely populated country in Europe, and its arable land even more densely populated than China's.[26]

In the 1840s an American parasite of the American potato, left behind when the potato crossed the Atlantic, caught up with its host, destroying crops across a wide breadth of northern Europe. The blight had dire effect, for instance, in Scotland and the Palatinate, but in no country was the effect as catastrophic as in Ireland. The story is one we all know, and there is no need to blaspheme it with repetition. The productivity, ease of cultivation, and wholesome nourishment of the American potato had beguiled the Irish into a Malthusian ambush. A million died in the famine, hundreds of thousands in ensuing epidemics, and hundreds of thousands of others fled over the Irish Sea and Atlantic. Within a generation following the 1841 census the population of Ireland dropped by half. (Incidentally, of all the foods sent to Ireland to relieve the starving masses, maize, being the cheapest nourishment available, was the most important.)[27]

Norway strayed halfway into the Malthusian cul-de-sac, and it is instructive to examine how that nation avoided disaster. There were a bit fewer than 900,000 Norwegians in 1815, and 1.7 million in 1865, products of one of the very highest annual growth rates in all of Europe. The vital role of potatoes in that growth spurt is certain, although the story is complicated by the spread of smallpox vaccination at the same time as potato cultivation. Informed and careful estimation sets the caloric value of the average

Norwegian's daily diet in 1800 at 1,800, and in 1855-1856 at 3,300. (The minimum requirement for the average man is 2,000 calories a day.) In that period potatoes spread from the south, where the tuber had first arrived about 1750, throughout the land. In 1809 the potato accounted for only 4 percent of the total food energy provision for Norwegians, and in 1835 for at least 28 percent. In the 1870s the annual per capita consumption of potatoes was 450 pounds, and that of grain only 420 pounds.

Norwegians, it would seem, were nearly as vulnerable to a failure of the potato harvest as the Irish. But they had no catastrophe because they were able to clear new lands, which slowed the subdivision of peasant plots, and utilized on the new lands new equipment and methods, increasing yields. This saved them from the penalties of dependence on the potato till mid-century, and after that industrialism and mass emigration relieved the population pressure in the rural areas. The Norwegians' chief advantage over the Irish seems to be in having entered the cul-de-sac later and, therefore, not having penetrated quite so deeply before advances in agricultural techniques, industrialism, and the possibilities of trans-Atlantic migration saved them from disaster.[28]

Rising standards of living have allowed Europeans in the twentieth century to make the choices about their diets—first the English working classes a century ago, and in our time the Romanians—and they have tended to return to their ancient staples, the small grains. There are exceptions, of course: the Finns are too far north to forgo the potato as a staple, and *polenta*, a constant in rural diet in northern Italy since the seventeenth century, is not going to disappear from dinner tables there. But the era of greatest European dependence on potatoes and maize seems to have passed, and we are now in a position to assess their significance in European history.

First, there is the matter of their influence on the population explosion that carried Europeans from 105 million in 1650 to 390 million in 1900. The two American staples without any doubt whatsoever were elements in that explosion—statistics on food production and consumption

prove that—but were they the cause? Causes are perhaps beyond the historian's ken. We can rarely declare with absolute confidence why people did what they did. Moreover, effects usually become causes and all is submerged under a swirl of feedback. Could not the same rise in numbers have been triggered by improvements in yields of traditional crops, from the rise in wealth that came with industrialism, and from such medical advances as smallpox vaccination?

That I very much doubt, especially for the North, because population increase preceded these developments in many places, but proof is, of course, impossible. I can only refer to what did actually happen, which is that many of the millions of the Europeans produced by the population explosion lived on potatoes and maize; and that these extraordinarily productive crops increased the production of other foods by releasing land for the small grains and vegetables, and for pasturage. To claim that the population explosion would have taken place without maize and potatoes strikes me as carrying counter-factual history further than it will stretch without breaking.

Europeans industrialized and vastly improved their lives materially in the two or three hundred years of maximum dependence on the Amerindian crops, changing human existence everywhere. Did maize and potatoes play a role in industrialization? The answer must be yes because industrialization drew millions of people out of agriculture, obliging those left behind to raise much more food per person than ever before. They met that obligation by increasing yields of traditional crops, and by resorting to the most productive food crops available to them, maize and potatoes. These became staples in the countryside, and necessities for many urban workers. For instance, let us consider the family, seven members, of a *skilled* and well-paid worker, Richard Goodwin of 45 Great Wild Street, London, in 1841. In an average week the staples of their diet consisted of twelve loaves of bread, which cost eight shillings, and eighteen pounds of potatoes, which cost only *nine pence.*[29] Friedrich Engels expressed the role of potatoes succinctly in his angriest book, *The Condition of the Working Class in England* (1845):[30]

The normal diet of the individual worker

naturally varies according to his wages. The better-paid workers—particularly when the whole family works in the factories—enjoy good food as long as they are in employment. They have meat every day and bacon and cheese for the evening meal. The lower-paid workers have meat only two or three times a week, and sometimes only on Sundays. The less meat they can afford, the more potatoes and bread they eat. Sometimes the meat consumed is cut down to a little chopped bacon mixed with the potatoes. The poorer workers can afford no meat at all and they eat cheese, bread, porridge, and potatoes. The poorest of all are the Irish, for whom potatoes are the staple diet.

The historian Sidney Pollard has called the Irish immigrants of that period "the mobile shock troops of the industrial revolution." They played the dismal role of enabling key areas in the British economy to grow without driving up the price of labor. In 1854 the Rev. A. Campbell of Liverpool wrote that in "the present state of the labour market English labour would be almost unpurchasable if it were not for the competition of Irish labour…"[31] Equivalent groups of poor men, women, and children played similar roles in the industrialization of other European nations, and in more cases than not, they depended on Amerindian foods as the core of their diets. Otherwise, they could not have been as usefully poor as they were, and not starved to death.

In the north of Europe potatoes were important not only in that they enabled the industrial workers to fill their stomachs with substance of rich caloric value and of some protein content, as well, but also of crucially important vitamin content. Potatoes had less vitamin C than fresh vegetables, fruits, and berries, but had the advantage of being available everyday throughout the winters. They saved multitudes from scurvy, one of the ancient curses of northern Europe. Even in relatively prosperous Great Britain in 1909-1949

potatoes supplied at least forty percent of the mean intake of vitamin C in working class households. Wherever and whenever potatoes were lacking in Great Britain because of Dickensian meanness, crop failures, or during wars when enemy blockades cut off the supplies, scurvy appeared—or we should say reappeared because it had been common among rural laborers before potatoes arrived.[32] Similar stories could be told of scurvy following potato shortages elsewhere.

Could there have been an industrial revolution in northern Europe without the potato? Probably, but that is not the way it happened, and all historians really have to deal with is what did happen. The early industrial workers fueled themselves with Amerindian foods, and without these the difficult transition from field to factory would have been slower and for many essential members of the labor pool perhaps fatal. Even with the potato, the urban poor tottered on the brink of intolerable malnutrition in the early decades of the new era. To illustrate, poor boys, fourteen to sixteen years in age, of London in the late eighteenth century and early nineteenth century ranged from about fifty-five to fifty-six inches in height. Of eighty-one ethnic groups for whom modern height data is available, only two, the desperately impoverished Lumi and Bundi of New Guinea, have shorter adolescents.[33]

Europeans industrialized and vastly improved their lives materially in the two or three hundred years of maximum dependence on the Amerindian crops, changing human existence everywhere.

The greatest significance of Amerindian crops in Europe's history is perhaps not merely—*merely*—

that they played important roles in the continent's population explosion and the industrial revolution. To appreciate their greatest significance we must pause to consider what is distinctive about Europe over the last six centuries. In that 600 years its people have experienced an enormous surge not only of numbers—from 60 million in 1400 to 390 million in 1900—but of economic growth, intellectual achievement, and material power. Other peoples have had similar surges—for instance, the Muslims in the early centuries of what Europeans call the Middle Ages, the Chinese of the Sung Dynasty—but their advances ended with general declines, economic and cultural. Thus far, Europe's surge is unique in its duration and promise of continuation.

Only once before in the last millennium has Europe had a surge comparable to the current one.[34] Between the ninth and fourteenth centuries Europe's population doubled and her people produced the high culture of the Middle Ages: scholastic philosophy, the Gothic cathedral, Dante, the mechanical clock, and the yeasty urban cultures of northern Italy and Flanders. The surge ended in the 1300s when Europe's population exceeded its capacity to feed itself and the Black Death arrived from the East, abruptly reducing the number of Europeans by about a third.

Europe's medieval surge lasted about three centuries, give or take a half century or so, before it collapsed. Three hundred years after that collapse, in the middle of the seventeenth century, Europe's population, which had been growing since some time in the fifteenth century, ceased to grow and even dipped down, especially in the Mediterranean and northwestern Europe, the most richly innovative regions of the continent. In the same period Europeans suffered what Paul Hazard has called the "crisis of the European consciousness," the kind of failure of nerve that often signals a downturn in a society's arc through time.

Precedent suggests that the seventeenth century decline in Europe's progress should have been a major decline, not to be nullified for generations. Instead it proved to be no more than a hitch in her progress. By the last decades of that century Europe's numbers were growing again,

and in the first decades of the next century economic expansion beyond previous levels was under way. Why? How? Luck played its part, of course. Barbarians did not sweep in from northern forests and eastern steppes to take advantage of Europe's weakness. The Turkish surge did not pass its previous high water mark at the gates of Vienna. The crisis did not include anything so horrendous as the arrival of the Black Death. The plague did take many lives in the seventeenth century, but by then Europeans knew in part how to limit its ravages or at least how to compensate for the lives and treasure it took. It disappeared from western Europe—forever, one hopes—early in the next century. (Carlo M. Cipolla suggests that in Italy maize, in a sense, replaced plague, providing food for those whom the disease would normally have carried off, and who, being "extra," would have starved without the new food.)[35] If cholera, Europe's next pestilential import from the East, had arrived in the seventeenth century, generations before scientists learned how to control it, the seventeenth century crisis might have been more profound.

There were immensely powerful positive factors, as well. By the time of the crisis of the 1700s Europe was in command in the Americas, and colonial gold and silver, goods, and markets helped to shorten the crisis; as did the profits from trade with West Africa and the Far East. The advance of European science, technology and the improvement of its administrative and financial techniques and institutions helped as well.

Let me also nominate Amerindian crops as a significant element in the recovery. In at least one way the seventeenth century crisis was similar to the fourteenth century crisis. Europe could not, with the agriculture it possessed, feed her lower classes and also support the high-flown schemes of her upper classes. Europe was deep into what might have been a major demographic decline when the Amerindian crops, adapted to European conditions and familiar to farmers in scattered areas, were ready for wide dissemination. Europe's farmers would, in time, greatly improve the yields they were able to obtain from their traditional crops and livestock, but what they needed in the seventeenth and early eighteenth centuries was an immediate miracle. That is what maize and potatoes supplied. When the pioneer of agricultural revolution, Viscount Charles "Turnip" Townshend, was born in 1674 European farming techniques were still primitive, but potatoes were already an essential food to considerable numbers of poor peasants in Ireland and here and there in the British Isles and on the Continent; and maize was a staple from Portugal to the Adriatic and becoming so in parts of the Danube basin and Balkans. In the late seventeenth and in the eighteenth centuries the Amerindian crops, though often cultivated by distinctly unscientific methods, provided what Folke Dovring has called "nutritional space," a delaying of disaster, a fending off of the Malthusian checks, until those tardy developments that historians have called the agricultural and industrial revolutions were under way.[36]

In the seventeenth century Europeans were able to "skip" a major crisis. In the eighteenth century Europeans were able to launch directly into massive and unprecedented advance from a plateau of capital, knowledge, intact infrastructure, and experience built up since the 1300s, rather than to stagger through additional years of crisis and *then* to begin yet more decades of struggle merely to regain what had been lost. For the first time in human history a people were able to break out of the cycle of advance and retreat, of ascent and crash, a cycle that matched every era of success with an era of dismay. We are at least partly in debt to the skills of Amerindian plant breeders for that breakout.

■

ENDNOTES

1. Jerome Cardano, *The Book of My Life*, translated by Jean Stoner (London: J.M. Dent and Sons, 1931), 189.

2. William Langer, "American Foods and Europe's Population Growth," *Journal of Social History*, VIII (Winter 1975): 52-4, 58; Alfred W. Crosby, *The Columbian Exchange: Biological and Cultural Consequences of 1492* (Westport: Greenwood Press, 1972), 171; *The Oxford Book of Food Plants* (London: Oxford University Press, 1969), 7-8, 177-8. See also Redcliffe Salaman, *The History and Social Influence of the Potato* (Cambridge: Cambridge University Press, 1985), *passim*; Nicholas P. Hardeman, *Shucks, Shocks and Hominy Blocks* (Baton Rouge: Louisiana State University Press, 1984), *passim*.

3. *Cambridge Economic History of Europe*, (Cambridge: Cambridge University Press, 1967), IV, 276-277; Antonello Gerbi, *Nature in the New World*, translated by Jeremy Moyle (Pittsburgh: University of Pittsburgh Press, 1985), 32, 189; *The Fontana Economic History of Europe: the Sixteenth and Seventeenth Centuries*, edited by Carlo M. Cipolla (Glasgow: William Collins and Co., 1974), 252,327-8; Langer, "American Foods," *Journal of Social History*, VIII (Winter 1975): 59.

4. *Hunger and History, the Impact of Changing Food Production and Consumption Patterns on Society*, edited by Robert I. Rotberg and Theodore K. Rabb (Cambridge: Cambridge University Press, 1983), *passim*.

5. Fernand Braudel, *The Structures of Everyday Life*, translated by Siân Reynolds (New York: Harper and Row, 1981), 74; for a general discussion of the subject, see *Hunger and History, the Impact of Changing Food Production and Consumption Patterns on History*, edited by Robert I. Rotberg and Theodore K. Rabb (Cambridge: Cambridge University Press, 1983).

6. *The Fontana Economic History of Europe, Sixteenth and Seventeenth Centuries*, 117.

7. *The Fontana Economic History of Europe, Sixteenth and Seventeenth Centuries*, 117, 311, 327, 464; Braudel, *Structures of Everyday Life*, I, 165-6; Langer, "American Foods," *Journal of Social History*, VIII, (Winter 1975): 59-60; Gionanni Levi, "Innovazione Tecnica e Resistenza Contadina: Il Mais nel Piemonte del 1600," *Quaderni Storici*, XIV (No. 3), 1092-1100; Troian Stoianovich and Georges C. Haupt, "Le Maïs dans les Balkans," *Annales*, XVII (January - February 1962): 84-93.

8. These and the other population numbers not specifically referenced in this article can be easily located in Colin McEvedy and Richard Jones, *Atlas of World Population History* (Hammondsworth: Penguin Books, 1978).

9. Langer, "American Foods," *Journal of Social History*, VIII (Winter 1975): 59-60; Paul M. Hohenberg, "Maize in French Agriculture," *Journal of European Economic History*, VII (Spring 1977): 68-9, 71; Alan S. Milward and S. B. Saul, *The Economic Development of Continental Europe, 1780-1870* (London: George Allen and Unwin, 1973), 78; Gauro Coppola, *Il Mais Nell'economia Agricola Lombarda (dal Secolo XVIII all'Unitá)*, (Bologna: Societa Editrice il Mulina, 1979), 145-47; Troian Stoianovich and Georges C. Haupt, "Le Maïs Arrive dans les Balkans," *Annales*, XVII (January–February 1962): 84-93.

10. Coppola, *Il Mais*, 154; Langer, "American Foods," *Journal of Social History*, VIII (Winter 1975): 60.

11. Beryl B. Simpson and Molly Conner-Ogorzaly, *Economic Botany, Plants in Our World* (New York: McGraw-Hill Book Co., 1986), 156-62; Graeme Barker, *Prehistoric Farming in Europe* (Cambridge: Cambridge University Press, 1985), 43-6.

12. J.G. Hawkes, "The History of the Potato," *Journal of the Royal Horticultural Society*, XCII (May 1967): 251; Mary Kilbourne Matossian, "Mold Poisoning and Population Growth in England and France, 1750 - 1850," *Journal of Economic History*, XLIV (September 1984): 673-4; see also Matossian, "Mold Poisoning: An Unrecognized English Health Problem, 1550-1800" *Medical History*, XV (1981), *passim* 73-84, and Matossian, *Ergot, Molds, and History*, forthcoming from Yale University Press.

13. J.G. Hawkes, "The History of the Potato," *Journal of the Royal Horticultural Society*, XCII (May 1967): 251-2, 255.

14. *Ibid*, 289-93.

15. *Ibid*, 291-3; Alain Molinier, "En Vivarais au XVIIIc Siécle: Une Croissance Démographique sans Révolution Agricole," *Annales du Midi*, XCII (1980), 301-15.

16. *Ibid*, 124, 225-8; Cecil Woodham-Smith, *The Great Hunger, Ireland 1845-1849*, (New York: The New American Library, 1964), 30; Langer, "American Foods," *Journal of Social History*, VIII (Winter 1975), 54.

17. Redcliffe Salaman, *The History and Social Influence of the Potato*, (Cambridge: Cambridge University Press, 1985), 238, 445-50.

18. *Ibid*, 54-6; William L. Langer, "Checks on Population Growth: 1750-1850," *Scientific American*, CCXXVI (February 1972): 99; *The German Peasantry, Conflict and Community in Rural Society from the Eighteenth to the Twentieth Centuries*, edited by Richard J. Evans and W.R. Lee (London: Croom Helm, 1986), 100 n61.

19. Alfred W. Crosby, *The Columbian Exchange: Biological and Cultural Consequences of 1492* (Westport, Conn.: Greenwood Press, 1972), 184.

20. Langer, "American Foods," *Journal of Social History*, VIII, (Winter 1975): 55; Gunnar Fridlizius, "Sweden," *European Demography and Economic*

Growth, edited by W.R. Lee (London: Croom Helm, 1979), 349; *Cambridge Economic History of Europe*, VII, Part I (Cambridge: Cambridge University Press, 1978), 430.

21. Crosby, *Columbian Exchange*, 184.

22. *The Fontana Economic History of Europe, The Industrial Revolution*, edited by Carlo M. Cipolla (Glasgow: William Collins Sons & Co., 1973), 130.

23. Hohenberg, "Maize," *Journal of European Economic History*, VI (Spring 1977): 99; Salaman, *History and Social Influence of the Potato*, 281-2.

24. Kenneth J. Carpenter, *Pellagra* (Stroudsburg, Pa.: Hutchinson Ross Publishing Co., 1981), xi, 2-3, 7, 31-2, 46, 48, 342; Coppola, *Il Mais*, 127-8; Jacques M. May, *The Ecology of Malnutrition in Central and Southeastern Europe* (New York: Hafner Publishing Co., 1966), 19, 40, 88, 147, 259.

25. Smith, Adam, *An Inquiry into the Nature and Causes of the Wealth of Nations* (New York: Modern Library, 1937), 161.

26. *Ibid*, 160; Langer, "American Foods," *Journal of Social History*, VII, 57; Woodham-Smith, *Great Hunger*, 26.

27. *German Peasantry*, 142; Salaman, *History and Social Influence of the Potato*, 291, 303-5, 315; Woodham-Smith, *Great Hunger*, 36, 48-51, 179-80; E.C. Large, *The Advance of the Fungi* (New York: Dover Publishers, 1962), 32, 35.

28. Michael Drake, *Population and Society in Norway, 1735-1865*, (Cambridge: Cambridge University Press, 1969), 41-74; Drake, "Norway," *European Demography and Economic Growth*, edited by W.R. Lee (London: Croom Helm, 1979), 293-4.

29. John Burnett, *Plenty and Want, a Social History of Diet in England from 1815 to the Present Day* (London: Scholar Press, 1979), 67.

30. Friedrich Engels, *The Condition of the Working Class in England*, translated by W.O. Henderson and W.H. Chaloner (Oxford: Basil Blackwell, 1958), 85.

31. Sidney Pollard, "Labour in Great Britain," *The Cambridge Economic History of Europe*, VII, Part I (Cambridge: Cambridge University Press, 1978), 113.

32. Kenneth J. Carpenter, *The History of Scurvy and Vitamin C* (Cambridge: Cambridge University Press, 1986), 101-3, 186, 224, 227.

33. Robert W. Fogel et al, "Secular Changes in American and British Stature and Nutrition," *Hunger and History, the Impact of Changing Food Production and Consumption Patterns on Society*, edited by Robert I. Rotberg and Theodore K. Rabb (Cambridge: Cambridge University Press, 1985), 270, 280.

34. Emmanuel Le Roy Ladurie's essay, "The Crisis and the Historian," found in the collection of his works entitled *The Mind and Method of the Historian*, translated by Siân Reynolds and Ben Reynolds (Chicago: University of Chicago Press, 1981) was the chief stimulus for the following discussion. Also, see E.J. Hobsbawm, "The General Crisis of the European Economy in the 17th Century" and "The Crisis of the 17th Century—II," *Past and Present*, No. 5 (May 1954): 33-53, and No. 6 (Nov. 1954): 44-65.

35. Carlo M. Cipolla, "Four Centuries of Italian Demographic Development," *Population in History, Essays in Historical Demography*, edited by D.V. Glass and D.E.C. Eversley (London: Edward Arnold, 1965), 575.

36. *Cambridge Economic History of Europe*, VI, Part II, edited by H.J. Habakkuk and M. Postan (Cambridge: Cambridge University Press, 1966), 634.